KOBI:
Memoirs of a Mustang

Copyright ©2014 by Heather Hamel

ISBN: 978-0-9972358-5-2

Cover by Sprinkles On Top Studios

Interior sketches by Jean Drayovitch

Published by Jakobi Publishing, LLC

Other books by Heather Hamel:

Horse Books:

Kobi: Memoirs of a Mustang

Sugar: My Journey Home

Ghostly Mysteries:

Murder of Crows

Destruction of Wild Cat (Halloween 2016 release)

Cryptozoology Series

Within Emerald Forests (Book 1)

Under Sapphire Skies (Book 2)

Beneath Diamond Waters (Book 3)

Across Ruby Fields (Book 4)

Contact Heather at: heather.hamel@hotmail.com
or through her website, www.HeatherHamel.com

Prologue

I have learned that there are three kinds of people in the world: the good, the bad, and the ignorant, the latter of which can be even worse than the bad.

I have also learned that most people have at least some good in them. It's the bad and the ignorant ones that you have to watch out for, and you can't always tell when you meet someone which kind of person they are.

This is *my* story, *my* journey, in which I have encounters with all those people: the good, the bad, and the ignorant. But don't worry; everything works out just fine.

After all, I am Kobi.

CHAPTER 1 — THE BEGINNING

One of my first memories is of running free alongside my mother, in a herd of wild mustangs, across the scorched earth of the Nevada plains. The wind tore through my mane and I ran faster and faster, hitting the ground hard as it thundered under my hooves. I squealed in delight and kicked up my hind legs as I ran. I felt wild, alive, and free.

"Keep up, son. You have to stay with the herd. Remember, there is safety in numbers." Mother urged me as she circled behind to nudge my hindquarters. "Get going."

You have never seen a prettier mare than Mother. She was dark bay, her coat a deep, dark brown, the color of the ground after the spring rains have soaked in. Her thick black mane reached down past her heavily muscled shoulders. Her tail was longer than most other mares' and brushed across the ground when she ran. She didn't have a single white mark on her. She was strong and powerful from running wild. She could move the fastest and the farthest in search of the most succulent green grass or cool blue water, which was why she was the lead mare in our herd.

Father was, of course, the only stallion for our herd of mares and yearlings, which included me and several of my half brothers and sisters. He was a handsome animal, the largest and thickest horse in our herd. His neck alone was thicker and more muscular than my chest. I hoped to be just like Father when I grew up: big, strong, dominant, and the leader of my own herd. We already looked identical; I was just a great deal smaller. We were both as black as a moonless, starless night, without a single white mark to distract the eye from our beautiful, pure color. While Father's forelock was so long and so thick you couldn't see his eyes, mine was just little tufts of frizzy black fuzz growing out of the top of my head. I had high hopes, though, that I would grow up to be just as striking as Father, if not more so!

Lost in my thoughts of becoming the greatest stallion in all of Nevada, I didn't notice that the herd had stopped to drink and I ran past the watering hole. I kept daydreaming and running for what seemed like miles. I was just enjoying being free. As my hooves drummed against the hard Nevada plains, I felt the vibration running up my legs with each stride. I kicked up so much dust that I couldn't see anything behind me. At first, I didn't realize that I was on my own.

I had run straight into the mouth of a canyon. I slowed to a trot to catch my breath as well as gather my bearings. I circled the inside of the canyon and turned around in order to head back out and rejoin my herd. Just then another horse caught my eye and stopped me in my tracks. Every muscle in my body tightened on alert: head up, neck tense, nostrils flared to catch any scents the wind might bring me. My entire body trembled with anticipation. I had never seen or smelled this horse before. Was he in our territory or had I ventured into his? I was much too young to be a threat to a grown stallion like this one, but it was still extremely dangerous for me to be in his territory.

My feet screamed "RUN!" but my mind wouldn't listen. I had spotted something else: that horse had an animal on his back. It was the size of a mountain lion, but it wasn't attacking the horse. The horse didn't appear to be in distress. He wasn't running, bucking, or screaming. No, he just stood still on the ridge and calmly watched me with this strange creature sitting on his back. Interesting, but I didn't want to waste any more time thinking about that. I had to leave. Getting out of there safely was more important than figuring out the strange creature.

My feet jumped into action, striking the earth in the same rhythm as my pounding heart. I ran faster and faster until I could see the canyon's opening getting bigger and bigger, closer and closer. I was almost out.

When I reached the mouth of the canyon, I saw a shadow pass across the entrance. Oh, no! What was that? Was it another stallion? Fear was starting to take over my senses. Then I heard a horse cry out and the shadow became a solid figure at the entrance: Mother!

I slowed to a trot as I approached her. "Where have you been?" she demanded as I came closer. She nipped me on the ear to chastise me. "I panicked when we stopped for water and you were nowhere to be found. You must always pay attention and stay with the herd. Stick together; there is always—"

"Safety in numbers. I know, I know, Mother," I was so relieved to be safe that I was a little sassy as I finished her sentence for her. She nipped me again for being disrespectful. My delight in seeing Mother made me forget all about the strange horse with the creature on its back.

Mother nudged me forward, "Don't ever do that again. Now we must get back. Your father is furious with you for not staying with the herd."

As we trotted back to the watering hole, Mother began lecturing me again on the dangers of going off alone. She had to be sure that I had learned my lesson. "You must stick with the herd. You don't want to end up like that little filly from last summer. She never got a second chance to learn her lesson that there is always safety in numbers."

The story about the filly going off by herself is one every newborn foal hears. She was a free spirit and didn't listen to the elder horses much. She was also a silly little filly with more dust in her head than smarts. She preferred playing, frolicking, and chasing butterflies at dusk instead of being safe. She was already weaned from her mother's milk and eating grass, but she was still much too young to not pay attention to where her mother was. Her fun and games took her away from the safety of the herd and too close to a cave where coyote pups were just learning to hunt.

Her mistake wouldn't have been deadly most of the time because horses are too big for a coyote to take down, but food had been scarce for them that year. They had begun to hunt in packs for larger prey, like a filly. She didn't stand a chance against them. They took her by surprise and had her throat in their powerful jaws before she could even whinny for help. Darkness had settled on the plains and it was morning before the herd found the lost filly—or what was left of her—from the coyote's feast.

I shuddered at the image in my head.

I was relieved when we finally rejoined our herd and I could put some distance between me and Mother's lectures, not to mention the gruesome retelling of the filly and coyote incident. On the trek back I decided not to trouble her any further, so I didn't question her about the strange horse I had seen. When we returned, though, I found Father and asked him about it. He was distraught by what I told him.

"Tell me again, son, how many horses were there?"

"One, but there was something on his back."

"Now, wait. Are you sure there was only *one* horse?"

"Yes, only one. Father, what was that on his back? It wasn't attacking him. It was just…I don't know…a strange creature." I mumbled, becoming more confused the more I thought about it. Maybe my eyes had played tricks on me. Maybe I wasn't remembering all of the details right. Maybe there wasn't another animal on the horse's back.

"It was a human," said Father.

"What's a human?" I asked.

"A predator. Humans are, by far, the worst predators that we have to fear. While a human has four legs, they walk on only two. This makes them move slower than us, so we can always outrun them, but they are smart and cunning. They can hunt us down more swiftly and surely than either coyotes or mountain lions can."

"But the horse didn't seem to be in any distress. Was he being attacked by a human and I just couldn't tell?"

"No, son. That horse had been tamed to allow a human to ride him like a beast of burden."

"Tamed? Ride him? But why?"

"The horse may have had no choice. At times, humans will chase us down and capture us. Then we only have two choices: let them dominate us and we can live, but by their rules, or fight back and probably die."

"Oh, that's horrible, Father. Which would you choose?"

"I would rather die than to allow a human up on my back. But come, son, I must get the herd moving again. That human you saw was searching for us. We must not let him find us."

With that said, we were on the move again before darkness fell across the plains. My thoughts, though, were on that horse, and humans.

*****

Soon the strange horse and his rider became a distant memory. My days were filled with running free with my herd, seeking out grazing lands and watering holes. Living the life of a wild mustang was all I craved.

Life went on this way into a second winter. Somehow, though, I knew things would have to change soon. I was becoming a grown stallion in my own right and knew there could only be one stallion in a single herd. Without a doubt, that stallion was Father.

One gray evening, Mother trudged towards me through the knee-deep snow, heavy with foal. "Son, you are almost fully grown; you are nearly as tall as I, and you have a long tail now instead of baby's fuzz. In spring, when the snow melts, all of the new foals will be born, and it will be time for you to leave with the other bachelors to create your own herds.

"But I don't want to go. I want to stay with you and Father. I'm not ready to be on my own yet!" I shook my head in frustration.

"Oh, yes, you are," she replied as calmly as only Mother could. "I know you are frightened, but I'm telling you this now so you can observe and learn as much as you can from your father and me before the time comes for you to go off on your own." She nuzzled me on my forehead and nipped affectionately at my withers before she headed off to go rest with the other mares, all of whom were heavy with foal.

I was furious and a little hurt. I always knew I would have to leave my Father's herd when I got older, but I just didn't think it would happen so soon. You never want to hear your Mother tell you that you have to leave home, either. I needed time to think and figure out what I was going to do, so I started running.

At first, I galloped as fast as I could and felt the cold wind whip through my mane and burn away all of my rage and frustration as my hooves tore through the snow. I tried to forget that soon I would have to find my own range and my own herd.

Once I had spent most of my anger and started to calm down, I heard a blood-chilling sound from my distant left.

Awoooooooooooooo.

Coyote!

Then from my far right, I heard an answering howl.

Awoooooooooooooo.

Coyotes!

I stopped in my tracks and swiveled my ears around as I tried to locate the coyotes. I flared my nostrils and blew hard trying to catch their odor. My neck was tense and my head high. Looking, I saw nothing. I heard nothing. I smelled nothing. They must not be too close, but they were out there waiting, and had caught my scent. My mind went to the story about the poor filly. I shook my head to clear it. They must not catch me by surprise.

Awoooooooooooooo.

The howl came from in front of me and was answered quickly by two more howls on each side of me.

Awoooooooooooooo.

They were closer now!

That only left one direction without coyotes. *Behind me.* I spun around to head back in the direction I had come. Then I saw them: a pack of five coyotes trotting after me. Stalking me. Sizing me up.

I ran faster. Not to be denied a meal for their pack, the coyotes ran faster too and closed the gap between us.

I was not going to go down easily. Without needing to turn my head, I caught a glimpse of my closest attacker. He was gray, the color of dirty snow. He kept his tail close to the ground as he ran, looking as if he would spring on me at any time. I also noticed that he wasn't large. He came up roughly to my knees. I could handle him. I knew since they are so small, coyotes are usually not a threat to horses if they are hunting by themselves. However, they made up for their size by hunting in packs to bring down larger prey–like me.

This was a pack.

The gray coyote came closer. Before he could pounce on me, I slowed down for a split-second and kicked out my hind foot with all my force, energy, and anger. I sent the coyote flying back into the snow.

I heard him scream. *Ieeee! Ieee! Ieee!*

I didn't stop running to see if he quit following me, but from his cries of pain I could tell that he wouldn't be chasing me anymore. I didn't know if the other coyotes in the pack would abandon the chase or double their efforts with one down, so I kept going as fast as I could.

The coyotes answered my question by staying close without breaking their stride. Another gray coyote made his move before I was able to put much distance between me and the remainder of the pack. From my side vision I saw him leap at me, but not towards my hind-quarters, as the last coyote did. This one was leaping toward my throat. I couldn't kick at him, but I could stop. Quick. The coyote didn't expect me to stop, so his leap was too far in front of me. He fell hard to the ground. I started running again and stepped on his chest. I felt it snap under my hooves but I didn't slow down. I was at full speed again before another coyote could take up the chase.

I wasn't going to slow my speed again for anything. It was a matter of life or death. Mine! I ran until I thought the coyotes had given up and then I ran some more. I ran until I had safely rejoined my herd. By the time I saw their outlines resting for the evening, I knew I had lost those predator coyotes. Mother was right: there *was* safety in numbers.

I thought my deep wheezing breaths might give away that I had been running hard, but not a single horse stirred. Not even Father, who was guarding over the herd, gave me a second glance. I was home and safe. When my heart stopped pounding and my breathing came easier, I tried to get some rest.

That night, though, sleep didn't come easy. Every time I heard a lone coyote's howl my heart started racing again. Whenever I managed to doze off I was jolted awake by the thought of having to leave the only herd I had ever known.

I had no idea I would be leaving much sooner than Mother or I had ever imagined.

CHAPTER 2 — THE CAPTURE

The sun rose the next morning on a day that was as cold, dark, and gloomy as my mood. A thick haze covered the plains and snow hung heavy in the clouds. It was only a matter of time until it fell again. I could see the other horses only as fuzzy shapes in the distance, although I could identify them by their unique, individual scent. I saw Father travel through the herd and check on everyone. He nudged all the horses together into a smaller, tighter group. That meant there was danger surrounding us. You could feel it electrify the air, but in the thick haze it was hard to tell which direction it came from.

Then we heard it. At first it sounded like thunder rolling in, but that couldn't be right since it didn't usually thunder when it snowed. Father heard it, too. He kept leaving the herd and dashing up on the ridge in search of the unknown threat. After scanning the horizon for a few minutes, he'd gallop back down to us to ensure that we were still safe, secure, and all packed together. Then he would run back up on the ridge.

The thunderous noise kept coming closer. One of the yearlings thought it might be another herd, galloping into our territory. His mother scoffed at the idea. "Your father has never let a renegade herd into our territory. He's not about to start now."

As soon as she said that, Father came galloping back down from the ridge, screaming only one word as he passed us. "RUN!"

We didn't have time to question or even wonder about his demand. Above the ridge where he had just stood rose an enormous bird with its wings flapping mightily to reveal the source of the thunder.

It wasn't any kind of bird I had ever seen before. It had no feathers, was too shiny, and too large to belong in the Nevada plains. Maybe it wasn't a bird at all; maybe it was a gigantic dragonfly. It had huge bulging eyes on top of its head and its wings were on top instead of being out to the sides. Whether it was an enormous bird or gigantic dragonfly, it was terrifying. It was time to run.

Its wings created such a fierce wind that our manes blew back and away from our necks as we tried to run away as fast as our hooves would carry us. Some of the yearlings' entire bodies were blown back. It was all they could do to stay on their feet. They were almost running backwards just to keep up.

Without hesitation, we ran as Father commanded and followed him at a dead gallop. My heart pounded in fast rhythm with my hooves. At first, we stayed together in a tight band, feeding off of each other's terror, driving forward as fast as we could go. Within minutes the pregnant mares started to fall back, followed by the yearlings with their mares, and then some of the older ones.

The creature followed us while spinning the air and the snow around us. This made it difficult for us to see where we were running. For some reason, though, it didn't attack any of the slower horses that fell behind, which surprised me. Every prey animal that I've ever seen would have singled out the weakest horse and moved in for the kill. They would've left the rest of us alone to escape, but this one didn't. It was strange. I shook my head to clear up all these thoughts that were causing me to slow down. When I caught up with Father, I was able to ask what was happening.

"Humans! They have found us. We must run until they leave."

"Why?" I screamed, even more panicked. "What do humans want with us?" I was so scared even my ears were shaking.

"I don't know." Father yelled back, terrified to the point that the whites of his eyes were showing.

If Father was that scared, this couldn't be good for the herd, since he was always known for becoming angry before he became fearful.

"Humans tried to get us once before, long before you were born," he huffed. "We outsmarted them then and we can do it again now." He dropped his head and began running even faster. Turning his head to look back at me, he yelled, "I'm going to check up ahead. Your job is to keep everyone moving. Look after the others. I will be right back."

With that said, he charged ahead and I took on his job of leading the herd. I slowed my pace down slightly, circling the herd, nudging them back together, remembering what Mother taught me, "Stay with the herd and stick together. There is always safety in numbers."

The enormous bird, which Father just told me were the humans, kept following us. Sometimes it circled us and other times it slowed down a bit, but it always stayed behind and drove us forward with its fury of wind. Never did it make a move to strike. It just seemed to want to linger behind and follow us. Strange as it was, there was no time to think about this dangerous predator who could change its shape when it wanted, yet not attack its prey.

With the entire herd close together, we kept running to the edge of our territory until we were about to enter into another herd's area. I could hear everyone behind me breathing heavily and starting to slow down even more. "No!" I screamed, "Run! Father said we must keep running." I strained my ears behind me, struggling to hear if the humans were also tiring. I couldn't hear any signs of them slowing.

"We can't keep going," Mother yelled. Her breathing was short and labored and sweat drenched her heavy sides. "We're losing our breath; our legs are about to collapse!" I understood what Mother meant. My own lungs felt like they were on fire and my breath came in short bursts. My legs felt as if they would

17

shatter into a thousand pieces at any moment and my heart pounded so hard I was afraid it might burst. We couldn't keep this pace up much longer. *Run!* Pure terror kept us moving. *Run!* We knew we were running for our lives. Somehow, we had to escape this predator, this predator called human.

Father came thundering up from the side just then. "This way! They won't be able to follow us down here." He had spotted a canyon where the sides dropped away to thin air. He led us all down and away from the humans.

The footing was rough. Rocks kept rattling loose from under my hooves, making me slip and scurry to stay on my feet. Father slid on some loose stones but luckily he kept his balance. He slowed us down to a trot and allowed us to pick the safest path to descend without risking a broken leg. It gave the herd a chance to catch its breath. A little rest from the breakneck pace we had been keeping was all we needed.

As soon as everyone was on flat ground again, we trotted deeper and deeper into a narrow valley. The canyon walls rose up above us and surrounded us on three sides. Father was right; the humans weren't able to follow us. We felt safe again.

We slowed our pace even further. My breathing came easier and deeper and my lungs stopped burning. My legs, while tired, could have kept this pace for the rest of the day if I needed to.

Up ahead stood a lone horse who watched us as if he was waiting for us to join him. He sprinted out ahead just before Father reached the horse. Father started our herd galloping again to catch up. Before he could talk to the outsider to find out what was going on, though, we came to a fork in the canyon. The strange horse veered sharply to the left and we followed.

Father didn't know he was leading us straight into a trap until it was too late. The canyon walls drew tighter and tighter, funneling us in. The path became so narrow that we were now running single file: first the strange horse, then Father, me, Mother, and the rest of the herd. The path twisted and turned until finally the canyon walls opened back up and the herd was together again. Only the path had ended. We were caught in a box canyon! Father roared in anger, reared up, and spun around. He was ready to lead us all back out to safety.

Then an enormous tree, even taller than Father, slammed across the opening, closing us inside. We were trapped!

Father screamed and again reared up to the sky. As soon as his front feet hit the ground again he backed up to get a running start and tried to leap over the barrier that blocked us. He threw his body up as high as he could, but it was no use. The barrier was so tall that Father's legs could never clear it. His body slammed to the ground with a heart-stopping *THUMP*!

Slowly, painfully, Father got back on his feet. He shook his head violently to clear it from the fall. That's when we noticed his nose was dripping blood either from hitting the wall so hard or the ground even harder. *Poor Father.* He dropped his bloody nose to the ground. He had led us straight into the human's trap, and he couldn't get us out. I had never seen my father so sad, so defeated.

*****

I learned a great deal over the next couple of days. I found out that humans were incredible predators, just as Father had said. Not only did they walk upright on two legs, but they could also turn themselves into a bird or dragonfly to chase us into a trap and capture us. I also found out the horse we followed was what Father called a "Judas" horse. It was an animal trained to do exactly what he did: deceive us, trap us. He was a wild mustang who had been caught, tamed, and trained by humans. Part of his training involved joining up with herds of wild horses and then leading them right into the humans' corrals. This Judas horse was very well trained. He betrayed us without a second thought.

The first thing the humans did was to separate us into small groups. They chased us around with sticks that had something white tied to the end that made *a lot* of noise. It sounded as if I had come across hundreds of Western Diamondback rattlesnakes at once. It was enough to scare all of us horses to run. As we ran around, they created openings in the walls and then shook their sticks as if they were going to attack us, but it was just to scare us into running into new traps. They closed the walls behind us as soon as we were inside one. Our entire herd was split apart. Mother was with the other mares, the yearlings were kept together but away from their mothers, and the group of stallions, including Father and me, were put in one trap together.

It was terrifying at first. I had never been away from Mother for this long. While I couldn't see her anymore, I knew she was around because I could still smell her. Any time that I became sad, all I had to do was take in a deep, deep breath and catch Mother's scent. It wasn't much, but it was all I had during those first few days. Her scent comforted me. I knew Mother was nearby.

After that, life became a blur. I was shifted from trap to trap, eventually separated from Father and then losing the scent of both Mother and Father. I was all alone for the first time in my life. With no one I knew around, I started watching the humans. They communicated in a language I had never heard before. To me they sounded like birds squawking as they circled the traps we were in and gestured to one another with noises and movements.

I studied their strange language and gestures in an attempt to learn and figure out these new predators as best I could. It was only after listening and watching for a while that I was able to learn the basics of their language. With careful study, I quickly understood human language almost as well as the speech of other animals.

Then came a day I won't soon forget. As the sun rose one morning, I noticed all of the humans were running around like ants whose mound had been disturbed. They were much more energetic than usual. They stood in small groups and gestured wildly towards the enclosures where all of us horses were kept. One group of humans started moving over toward the stallions, carrying their sticks with the loud, white things at the ends. As they came closer, they started moving their sticks to get the noise started. This, of course, got me and every horse moving as far away from them as we could. That noise was awful!

We stirred around in the tight space, shifting to one side only to see a human with his noisemaker approaching, which made us shift back to the other side. They kept moving us around like that until one of the horses spotted an opening in the enclosure and headed for it. He escaped, and after seeing him escape, we all immediately ran out behind him. *Freedom!*

But no, it wasn't an escape. It was another trap.

The humans had successfully herded us once more. This time we were wedged, one horse at a time, between two walls. My nose was pressed into the horse's tail in front of me, just like the horse behind me had his nose in my tail. Tail to nose, and nose to tail. It wasn't comfortable. We would inch forward ever so slowly and then stop, only to inch forward again. We were in line for what seemed like an eternity as we crept slowly toward the unknown. Panic and anxiety started to spread through us like wildfire. Finally, the tail in front of me was gone and - freedom! I saw freedom!

I leapt forward and then above all of the other sounds of the day, I heard a loud *CLICK*! My forward motion stopped immediately. My ribs and shoulders were squeezed tight on both sides. I tossed my head up to try to fling myself backward out of the trap but I couldn't. I could barely lift or turn my head. I panicked.

"Easy, boy." One of the humans said. I pushed myself frantically around, unable to move much in any direction.

"Calm down and it will all be over soon."

I was outraged at being caught again but I realized fighting was useless. I could neither move nor wiggle my hindquarters. I couldn't even twitch my skin to make the flies move. I knew I wouldn't be able to go anywhere unless the humans allowed me.

Next, I felt their hands around my face. They opened my lips and grabbed my tongue! They moved my tongue from side to side. I thought it was going to rip free. Those humans smelled awful and their hands left the worst taste I had ever had in my mouth. Once they let my tongue go free, I tried to spit out their taste.

"This one's about two." I heard one say.

I had no idea what he was talking about and why he thought there were two of us in here. I was obviously the only horse in this tight enclosure.

"Yes, that's right, he's two," another said.

But before I could figure out what they meant, something was stuck in between my lips and shot an unbelievably foul substance into my mouth. I tried spitting it out, but the human held my mouth closed until I had swallowed. The taste made me gag. And I had thought humans tasted bad!

"Alright, this one's been de-wormed," one of the humans said. "Hand me the vaccines."

Worms? What was he talking about? Who has worms? I don't have worms! And what are vaccines? What are they doing to me?

The human put his hand on my neck and immediately a wasp stung me. I wanted to move my head around to dislodge the wasp from my neck, but movement was a waste of time. Right away several more wasps got their stingers into my neck. Ouch! I couldn't stop them, either. I never figured out what a vaccine was, but I won't forget the swarm of wasps that attacked me that day.

It was after the stinging stopped I actually heard the wasps. All the buzzing, there must have been hundreds of them! I could feel them humming and buzzing down the crest of my neck. This time they kept their stingers to themselves. The humans wiped something on my neck in the exact same spot that was just buzzing and humming.

All of a sudden, that spot was freezing cold as if I were rolling in the snow. Fortunately, the sensation lasted only a few moments.

"Okay. He's all done: de-wormed, vaccinated, and freeze branded."

"What's his ID number?"

"Number 02585761. All ready for the next one."

The pressure on my ribs released and I could breathe freely again. I tested to see if I could move my neck up and my feet forward. I could! As soon as I found I could, I darted out of the chute and into the enclosure with my newest herd, hoping I was all done with humans.

Father was right: humans were fearsome predators.

CHAPTER 3 — ON THE MOVE

Humans. They stayed away. I began living a fairly uneventful life with my new herd, eating dried grass and drinking from small ponds until the days became long and warm again. One morning, though, before the sun was fully up, there were humans swarming all over the place. I sensed there was change in the air again; you could always smell it on the humans whenever things were about to change.

The humans started moving us around the way they always do and shaking their loud sticks. We moved! As soon as they had us over to one side of the pen, they shifted the barriers over to the other side. They created a narrow path that led to a large silver cave. Not a single one of us wanted to be the first horse down that path. Certainly not me! The mouth of the cave was huge and dark. There was no way of telling if mountain lions, coyotes, or any other creatures waited for us in there, ready to attack.

Since none of us would head for the cave, the humans surrounded us and herded us toward the walled path they had created, shaking those loud sticks the entire time. They closed in on us, leaving us no choice but to move onto their path. As soon as the last horse was in line, they closed the path behind us, leaving only one way to go: right into the cave. There was no way I was going to go in there. No! It was dark and scary. Even so, the horse behind me kept pushing me forward and ever closer to the unknown.

When I reached the front of the line, I had no choice but to step up and enter the cave. It wasn't as dark as I had thought. There were openings in the walls that let the sun in and let the wind pass through. It was tight, though, with all of the other horses in there. We were pushed and shoved as each horse entered. Finally the last horse was inside. They closed the opening to the cave with a loud *CLICK*. That noise again! My heart sank. Every time I heard that sound, my life changed somehow. For the worse.

As I wondered about my life changing yet again, I felt the ground beneath my hooves start to move. We were moving! We were packed in so tightly that I had no fear of falling from the all twists and turns the cave took. I had horses holding me up on all sides. It felt as if the cave around us moved forever. When it became dark outside, we were still moving. When the sun rose the next morning we were still moving. I didn't think we would ever stop, but we finally did.

"Alright boys, you're here. Hutchinson Correctional Facility. Everybody off."

The cave door opened. We saw nothing new, just another dry, sandy lot. The only way I knew we were in a different place was the air. It smelled different and had a charge which made me want to get away. Even the humans smelled different, they had a coarseness about them, that I had not encountered before. I didn't like it.

Everywhere I looked, I saw either a horse or a human; there was nothing else to see. Some humans had those noisy sticks and started shaking them around to get us to start moving. As always, we moved. As we were darting about, I could hear the humans yell, "That's the one," or "I'll take *him*." Then the horse they had yelled about would be maneuvered until he was alone, then put into a separate pen, away from the main herd.

Then, close by, I heard, "I'll take that one; the black one. He's small and wiry, just like me." At first I didn't think it was possible they were talking about me. I may be many things, but I'm not small. They couldn't be talking about me. But then the other horses started shifting away from me, so I knew it must be me. They moved me back and forth around the pen with their sticks until I wound up in a smaller area with a couple dozen other horses.

By sunset, all of the horses who had not been chosen were loaded back into the moving cave, and they left. Now, I found myself in a much smaller herd than when I had started the day. We were given a small pond to drink from and some dry grass to eat. Then the humans went away for the night. I was glad. I needed a rest and some time without humans around.

I lifted my nose in the air and inhaled deeply. I didn't catch a hint of Mother or Father's scent. I had not seen or smelled them for a long time. I wondered where they were, if they were alright, and if Father had managed to free them. I shifted around to try getting comfortable and bumped into another horse with my rump. He nickered in response and sought comfort from our closeness. I did the same. I rubbed up next to him for the night, feeling his rough coat and thinking of my old herd.

The next day all the horses were separated. Our new pens were tiny: I couldn't run more than five or six paces in any direction. The only way I could get a good run was to circle around the walls on the inside of my pen. Even then, I had to go around several times before my legs would begin to burn. I was given my own very small pond to drink from, but it was only big enough to put my nose in. I emptied it several times a day. I was

29

also given my own pile of dry grass to eat. It was nice to have it all to myself, without having to defend my food or water from another horse, but on the other hand, I wasn't able to get any extra food by chasing off another horse so I could enjoy theirs.

Before long, a human joined me. He was small, skinny, and smelled sour from sweat and fear. His eyes were wide as he looked at me, and his movements were quick and jerky. He was unlike the humans I had known before; they usually smelled like dirt and dried grass, and moved with slow confidence.

"Alright, Wade," another human yelled to him from outside the pen. "Keep your head down and don't look at him. Walk slowly toward the empty bucket. Good, good. Now, turn the bucket over and sit on it."

So that's what those little ponds are called: buckets!

The directions kept coming. "Keep your back to him. Slouch down a little. That's it. Be friendly. Make yourself as non-threatening to him as you can. Remember, they are flight animals, and to them we are predators. Good! Now just sit there until he comes to you. I'll come back later to check on your progress. Oh, and feel free to talk to him. He needs to get used to our voices."

I turned to look at Wade's back. He didn't look like anything to be afraid of, but he didn't look like anything to interest me either. I ignored him and munched away on my dried grass. I walked over to take a drink. Wade didn't move. He just kept sitting there, head down. He may have even been asleep for all I knew. The longer he ignored me, the madder I got. I was here because he picked me out of the herd, and now he was going to sit with his back to me.

I figured I could do the same to him, I moved around to where I could still eat my dried grass, but put my hindquarters to his back.

While we waited, back to back, the sun rose higher in the sky. "Well, Wade, how's it going?" The other human had returned.

"Slow. He doesn't seem to be afraid of me, but he doesn't seem to have much need for me either. He's just not interested."

"Well, you might just need to wait him out. He'll get curious about you soon enough. Have you been talking to him?

"No. I don't know what to say to a horse."

"It doesn't matter what you say, he won't understand you anyway. Just let him hear your voice. Maybe it will pique his curiosity."

Now, just wait a minute! Who says I wouldn't understand what Wade said? Ignorant humans! I understand what you're saying. I just don't care about it.

"Alright, I'll give it a shot. It's gotta be better than just sittin' here."

31

"Well, boy," Wade said. "You and I are a lot alike. We both used to be wild and free and now neither one of us is. I got thrown in this jail because I was a little too wild, and a little too stupid, and did some bad things. That's my fault. But it's not your fault you're in here; you just didn't run fast enough. As soon as you learn you can trust me, I'll show you humans can be good to you and maybe, just maybe, you'll be able to find a good home someplace."

*****

Things went slowly for Wade and me for the first couple of days. After Wade was told I wouldn't understand him, he told me his life story. I just listened to him while I chewed my dried grass. He told me about his beginning. His parents fought all the time. They didn't seem to care one way or another what happened to him, so he turned to lying and stealing to get the things he needed to survive.

Now, Wade, that's the problem. Humans need to be more like horses. Horses are always honest with each other. I can't understand why you would do such a bad thing like lying, but I do understand stealing if no one was looking, like getting an extra meal from another horse. Too bad you can't understand me. I could teach you a great deal about life.

Wade told me he kept doing more and more bad things until he ended up in here, the Hutchinson Correctional Facility, as an inmate. Wade told me that I was actually part of the plan to help him show he was ready to be set free again. By learning to gain my trust, he would learn how to get other humans to trust him. By training me, he would learn skills for working with another living being.

After listening to his stories, I decided to help him. He wasn't a bad human, he had just done some stupid things, and made some foolish choices. I knew teaching Wade wouldn't be easy, but if either one of us ever hoped to get out of this place, then I would have to take the first step. So I did.

The next morning, while Wade was talking to me, I walked up behind him and gently nudged his shoulder. I heard him take in a quick breath. I tossed my nose up and got ready to bolt in the opposite direction, but he made no motion to move or turn around. He held his breath, but ignored me. So I nudged him again. This time I used my lip to feel his neck and ears. What a strange feeling that was. Since he let me do it, and didn't make any sudden moves, I kept exploring my new human. This was kinda fun!

Up close, Wade's scent was nothing I had ever smelled before. It was an interesting mixture of dirt, sweat, horses, with a hint of something sweet. The skin on his neck was dry and tough, like mine from the late summer sun. His short hair was coarse and tickled my lip. I sneezed and took a step back.

Slowly Wade turned around. He didn't try to challenge me or look directly at me. He kept his head down and started whispering. "That's it. See? I'm not going to hurt you. Good boy!" He raised his arm too fast and I quickly backed out of range. I wasn't ready for him to move so suddenly. "That's ok. We'll get there."

Over the next few days, Wade kept coming and telling me stories. I would go up to him and occasionally nudge him, and the next time he reached out to me, I was ready for it. I let him touch me. Hmm. A little strange, but nothing bad happened. My skin didn't burn or freeze from his touch and while I would have preferred to have been groomed by another horse, this wasn't so bad. He rubbed my shoulders and then moved up to my withers. By the end of the day, I had allowed him to scratch all of those itchy spots I seemed to have all the way up to my ears.

After getting to know Wade through the stories he shared with me, and watching him grow more comfortable within his own skin by working with me, I realized I didn't mind spending time with him. I still would rather be with my own herd back in Nevada, but since I didn't think I would ever see my parents again or find my way back to my home range, Wade would have to satisfy my need for a companion. I know I had been chosen by a kind human. Things could have been worse. I could hear some of the other humans raise their voices to the horses and yell at them. I knew Wade would never do that to me.

The next morning, Wade brought something in the pen with him, something long, thin, and twisted together. It was a tangled mess. As I walked up to him, he held it up so I could smell it. "This is a halter," he said, "I have to teach you to wear this. After that, we can work on leading and tying. But this is the first step."

I was curious and a bit nervous as to what he had in mind. He began to fit the halter over my muzzle. I started backing up; I didn't know if I really wanted my nose in that thing. Every step I took backward, Wade matched it with a step forward, keeping the halter loosely around my nose. When my rump hit the fence and I couldn't move back anymore, Wade seemed to sense I was getting uncomfortable and he dropped his hands, removing the halter from my nose so I wouldn't panic. He turned and walked away, giving me some space to move again.

Wade waited, with his back turned to me, until I was ready to return to him. When I did, I allowed him to slip the halter back over my nose. I didn't back up this time, I just stood still. He placed the top of the halter over my ears, where he had scratched me dozens of times before. I didn't move. He tied the two pieces together and backed away, leaving me wearing the halter on my head.

35

"Now look at what a handsome boy you are."

Me? Handsome?

"You get to wear this all day today and all night tonight, to get used to the feel of it. But be careful when you walk around and try not to step on the lead rope."

Try not to step on the what? My head was quickly snatched down. I tried to lift my head but it wouldn't budge. I started to get scared. Why couldn't I move my head? I reared up, and released my head again.

Wade started laughing. "I told you to watch out for the lead rope! It'll get you every time."

I learned quickly that when I was wearing the halter I should walk slowly. That way if I stepped on the lead rope it wouldn't catch me by surprise and jerk my head down.

The next morning, when Wade came in to see me, he spent a great deal of time just rubbing his hands down my neck, withers, rump, and legs. It felt so good to be groomed. It almost reminded me of being back with Mother. She had groomed me like that, too, but with nuzzles and nips. When Wade reached my face and head, he rubbed my ears, then around my eyes, and finally my muzzle. Once he had me completely relaxed, he practiced taking the halter on and off of my head. I was in such a calm state that I didn't think twice about what he was doing. It was all good!

"Alright, my little prison pony. Today we're going to start taking you around with the lead rope."

As soon as the words were out of his mouth, I felt a gentle, constant pressure on the side of my nose. I tipped my nose in his direction and released some of the force.

"Good boy! Now let's see if we can get those feet moving in this direction too."

I started feeling a little more pressure on my nose. It didn't hurt, but he was using enough force for me to think I knew what he wanted. I sidestepped one step in his direction.

"That's it!" Wade startled me. He came up and started rubbing my neck. "Let's try the other side."

I found that it was much easier to do what he had asked, and to yield to the pressure when he switched over since I knew that's what he wanted. He was so pleased with me that he kept the day's session short.

"You're doing so well that I want to end this on a positive note." Wade threw me some extra dried grass. "You worked hard today!"

The next day Wade tried to teach me to walk right beside him while he held the lead rope. I had no idea what he wanted. I knew how to walk by myself wearing a halter and I knew how to turn with Wade guiding me, but to walk beside him while he held my lead rope was a different level of challenge. At first, I couldn't do it. I froze and refused to take another step.

Wade sensed my confusion. He got a super long rope, one that was long enough to go all of the way around my body. He clipped one end to my halter and ran the rope behind my rump. He held onto the end of rope and used it to push me from behind and encourage me to walk with him.

I kept jumping ahead like a frog, trying to keep the rope away from my hindquarters. Wade kept up with me and before long, we were walking all of the way around the pen without a single hop. Now that I knew what he wanted, Wade clipped the regular lead rope back on my halter. I stayed right beside him. I figured it was much easier than having something around my butt the whole time.

After he had me walking beside him and turning when he asked, we moved on to "whoa." I soon found out "whoa" was just another word for stop. It was pretty easy to figure out after the first or second time, and I found out I didn't mind "whoa." It was the easiest thing we did together. I could stand there and do nothing just perfectly!

I was pleased and ready to move on to the next stage of Wade's training when he did something that surprised me. One day, after a really good session together, Wade came up and put his arms around my neck.

"Well, my little prison pony," he whispered into my mane, "I guess this is goodbye. I'm going to miss you, boy. Thanks to you and all of our progress together, I should be getting out of this place in a couple of days. After I'm gone, there won't be any reason for you to stick around either. You'll be sent out, too, with the next group of horses. You've taught me more than I taught you, and now that you're halter broke, I hope you'll find a really good home, one with really good people who will appreciate you for just being you."

I had no idea what Wade was talking about this time, but when he left that evening, my mane was damp from where he'd rested his head while he said his goodbye.

Wade wasn't as bad as he thought he was.

CHAPTER 4 — THE ADOPTION

After Wade left I found out he was right, there was no reason for me to stay in the Hutchinson Correctional Facility any longer. So when the next group of horses came through, I was loaded into their moving cave.

With a loud *CLICK*, I was off again. Another new life ahead of me!

Thankfully, this trip was very short. We rode a little while, were unloaded, and settled into a large field all before the sun went down.

This new pen was, by far, the largest I had been in since the humans captured me. There was grass as far as my eyes could see. I could run in almost any direction I wanted to and my legs would be burning, my heart pounding, and my breath coming in short gasps before I saw another barrier either too tall for me to jump over or too low for me to scoot under.

The humans left me and my new herd alone, mostly. They probably figured there was nothing else they could do to us, so they just let us be.

I was wrong again!

After the winter snows had begun to fall, the humans began scurrying about. At first I thought they were straddling small animals that were squat and low to the ground. Then I realized they weren't straddling animals. The humans had changed their shape again, like they had done before when they turned into the strange silver bird or large dragonfly.

This time, the creature the humans became closed in on us much too fast, faster than I'd ever seen an animal run. When one got closer, I saw it wasn't an animal. It didn't have a head or legs. And it was loud!

I've seen this before. Where? Think, think, think!

The sound made by the strange creature was one I was vaguely familiar with. It was somewhere between buzzing and growling. The closer it got towards us, the louder the growling became, forcing all of us horses to run like the wind to try and escape.

That's it! I saw them when I was with Wade. The humans rode them when they brought our dry grass and water to our

41

pens. They weren't dangerous then; they just helped the humans carry more food and move faster to feed us. But there's no food on them now, and they are moving way too fast this time. What are the humans up to now?

It wasn't too long before one of the horses in this new herd, one who had experienced this situation before, took the lead and started moving us all toward an opening in the field barriers. For the briefest of moments, I was transported back to the time when Father had us all following behind the Judas horse, changing all of our lives forever.

I don't have a good feeling about this.

I shook my head to break up those disturbing thoughts that were clinging to me like a spider's fine web.

We followed the lead horse through several fields, pursued by the humans and their small, swift, growling creatures. By the time the lead horse came to a stop, we once again found ourselves rounded up into a small pen. The walls were tight around us.

"I just knew it! A Judas horse!" I screamed in frustration. I decided right then and there I was not going to follow any more horses. From now on, I would be the leader of the herd or nothing.

"Alright boys, everybody on the trailer," yelled one of the humans as they herded us into yet another moving cave.

Anytime I found myself around a human, I paid careful attention to what they said so I was beginning to understand their language a little better. I thought it would be in my best interest to know what they were saying so I could figure them out and what they wanted with me. I understood now that when they talked about "trailers" they were going to put us in those silver caves and move us again. I wish they just would have said that from the beginning. I may have come willingly.

Probably not though. I wasn't ready to leave yet. So far this was the best place I had been since I was captured, and part of me wanted to stay here eating grass and spending time with my latest herd. On the other hand, another part of me wanted to continue this journey I had started, hoping at some point to be reunited with Mother or Father. While I was considering my options, I found myself being loaded on one of the waiting trailers.

So much for being a leader and not a follower! I need to learn to wait and think before I act.

CLICK!

This leg of the journey seemed to take forever. It was daylight when we started, but it soon became dark, which made the cool air around us even colder. But since there were so many horses huddled together in the trailer, we were able to keep each other warm. We travelled this way for another full day and night.

As soon as the sun started casting its light for the second time on this journey, we had stopped and the trailer doors opened.

As we came out, I noticed the air was nowhere near as cold as it had been when we were loaded up. I couldn't see the smoke coming from my nose when I breathed and my fluffy winter coat wasn't sticking straight out anymore. It was almost as if I walked on the trailer in winter and walked off in spring. I looked around trying to see and smell the signs of spring: the green buds on trees, or the sweet smell of tender shoots of grass. I was surprised to only see dirt and more pens.

As we walked off the trailer, there were barriers set up so that we were only able to travel in one direction, toward more waiting pens. Once there, they separated us into smaller pens to keep the stallions separated from the rest of the horses. I looked around, trying to catch a glimpse or scent from Mother, Father, or any of my former Nevada herd. I didn't recognize or smell anybody I knew from home. They were all strangers to me here.

After a long day of moving us around, I heard a human announce, "After we give this group of horses some hay and water, everyone can go home for the night. I expect to see everyone here bright and early tomorrow morning. We have a lot of horses to adopt out, and I'm imagining we are going to have a large crowd here tomorrow. It's been awhile since we've brought mustangs to Florida, and we always seem to do well here."

Then the humans started rushing about, making sure that each pen had hay and a few buckets of water. I wanted to know what "hay" was since I hadn't heard of it before. I was happy to see that hay was the name for enormous piles of dried grass. I was famished!

*****

That human was right. There was a crowd of humans as soon as the sun rose the next morning. Before long, there were at least four humans for every horse. They just milled about, looking at us in our pens, and then moving on to look at another pen of horses. Their constant talking was like buzzing in my ears. I kept trying to hear what they were saying, but all of their voices blended together into such a loud, droning sound I couldn't make out any individual words.

Before long, I noticed the same pair of humans kept coming back to my pen. They were talking about me. I made my way over to the fence beside them so I could try and figure out what was going on. The couple consisted of a smallish, wiry male, who reminded me a great deal of Wade, and a petite female. I pricked my ears in their direction. They smiled at me.

"But Danny, I really like this one." The female gestured to me. "He's the only one that's come up to the fence since we've

45

been here. All of the other horses run away as soon as we get close. He so handsome and seems so sweet. I think he likes us."

Handsome and sweet. That about sums me up!

"Alise," Danny said with a sigh. "We agreed that we weren't going to buy a horse today. We just came here to see them."

"But Danny…."

"No 'buts.' I have two horses at the house if you ever want to ride them."

"But I want my *own* horse. Lazy is your horse, and Loco is, well, crazy. They're no fun for me to ride. If I had my own horse, we could go riding together. It would be so much fun."

"No," Danny said. "We'll go through and look at the horses one more time and then we are leaving—without one. You can always ride Lazy when we get home. Leave this horse alone and please step away from the fence."

The couple meandered away. I saw the female, Alise, looking back at me and smiling each time she would approach another horse's pen. Eventually, they made their way back around to me.

"Oh, Danny, please, can we get him?"

"No."

"But didn't you hear what those guys over there said? What they said they were going to do with him? I just overheard that man over there saying that this one, number 5761, is going through his last roundup. He said that 5761 falls under the three strike rule. If this horse is not adopted by his third auction, then he's going to be put to sleep. And this is his third auction."

What? Why would they want to make me go to sleep? How long would I sleep for? I'm not really tired right now.

"What? No, now that just doesn't make any sense." Danny said. "Why in the world would they want to put him down?"

What? Now they want me to lie down? And go to sleep? This is crazy! Are you sure you heard them right?

"It doesn't make sense." Danny continued. "Why would they spend all of this money to capture him, vaccinate him, worm him, and have him halter broke, just to kill him?"

Kill who? Kill me?

I got a terrible knot in my stomach and my blood turned to ice in my veins.

Why would anyone want to kill me? I haven't done anything wrong.

I had to get out of here and fast. That female, Alise, was my only chance. I inched closer to the fence and stuck my nose through it, trying to reach her and give her a good nuzzle, like I used to give Wade.

Alise was crying now. "See, Danny, he wants to be with me. We have to take him home. We have to save him. Oh, pleeeease."

"Oh, for the love of...." Danny muttered. He seemed irritated now. "We don't even have a trailer here. We can't bring him home."

"I'm sure we can find someone willing to bring him home for us," Alise sniffled. "Please."

Danny muttered something under his breath. "Alright, I'll go see if I can find someone willing to trailer him to our place. If not, I'm sorry Alise, but you won't be able to rescue him."

"Thank you, Danny, you are the best!"

Yes, Danny. If you get me out of here, you are the best!

Danny seemed to be a little nervous and way too twitchy, like he had an itch inside him he just couldn't scratch, but if he could get me out of here, then he would definitely be the best human I had met so far. Wade had told me there were other good humans out there.

Danny must have been able to find a way to get me home since he and Alise were still hanging around when the auction started. When I heard, "Number 5761, black gelding from Nevada," the humans shook their loud sticks around me, making all the other horses move away, and chasing me into a smaller, tighter pen.

When I was alone and separated from the other horses, I looked around to find Danny and Alise. Now was their chance to get me out of here. After watching other horses going through this a few times ahead of me, I figured out what to expect when a human wanted to take a mustang away: they just raised their hand. I never understood why waving away flies allowed them to take a horse, but it did. If more than one human raised their hand for a horse, all the humans around them became excited, buzzing like bees. The longer the hands went up, the more excited everyone became. Humans have some unusual habits.

I found Danny in the crowd and expected to see his hand fly into the air. It didn't. Someone else's hand went up first to start me at $125. Alise elbowed Danny in his chest, making his hand shoot up, raising me up to $135. And that was it. The other person decided not to go any higher for me. The excitement quickly quieted down. I was sold for $135.

Humph, $135! I've seen other horses go much higher. In fact, I'm worth at least twice that!

Alise came running up to my pen. "We did it! You're safe and all mine. You're going home with me. You're just going to love it there."

"Now Alise, I just want to set the record straight while we're still here," Danny said. "I'm not sure what you overheard earlier, but the guys who work here said that there is no such thing as the three strike rule. You were either mistaken about what you heard, or he made the whole thing up. I hope you didn't make up that story just so I'd agree that you could have your own horse."

"Oh, then maybe I just misunderstood them." Alise waved her hand, dismissing Danny's comment. "Still, you have to admit it will be fun to ride our horses together. He *is* such a sweet and handsome boy, too, and he's all mine."

The humans with the loud sticks came by and spooked all of the horses that were in my pen. But the other horses seemed to know it was me they were after and they all ran to the other side of the enclosure, leaving me all alone.

It was my time to leave and I knew just what to do. I ran into the alley that would lead me into my next trailer, my next meal, my next home.

Right before I entered the trailer, someone cut the numbered auction tag from around my neck. Then they placed the brand new halter Alise had just bought on my head, shook the loud stick at me, and sent me into the trailer. I heard that familiar sound: *CLICK*! On to my next adventure.

CHAPTER 5 — MIDNIGHT

I was rattling around in the horse trailer by myself for what seemed like hours, with no other horses for company or support. After awhile it was difficult to stand up. I was tired of slamming into the sides of the trailer whenever Danny made a turn, banging my chest in the front of the trailer when he stopped, and crashing my rump into the back of the trailer when he moved again.

I was exhausted and scared of what would happen to me if I fell onto the floor. With no one there to help me get back up, I would be just rolling around back and forth knocking myself bloody and senseless.

Finally the trailer stopped and the roar of the truck quieted. I heard Danny and Alise's voices as they walked around to the back. The trailer hinges screamed as Danny opened the door, flooding the inside with light and making me jump. I didn't want to stay in that metal trailer one minute longer, but I didn't want to get out, either. This couldn't be my new home. I couldn't smell any grass, fresh or dry. All I could smell was dirt. Surely these humans must be confused by stopping here and making me get out. Why would we want to stay in a place with no food?

Danny wouldn't give up. The more insistent I became about staying in the trailer, the heavier his hands became to get me out. He shook the lead rope, shooting vibrations all the way to my chin. I threw my head up, banging into the roof. I dropped my head back down, shaking it, trying to get the buzzing in my ears to stop. I didn't notice that Danny had walked into the trailer to help encourage me to get out. He grabbed my lead rope. He shoved my nose to my chest, which knocked the breath out of me, and made me back up to get away from the pressure on my nose.

Before I knew what had happened, I had backed all of the way out of the trailer. When my feet hit solid ground again, I thought there must be some kind of mistake. I had been brought to a wasteland. This was no place for a horse to live. It was bigger than the pens back at the adoption roundup, but it was nowhere near as large as the plains of Nevada. It was a dry, sandy lot, kind of like Nevada, but there was no grass whatsoever where I was to be kept. The only grass I saw was *outside* the fence. There were several old, beaten up vehicles in the fenced area along with an old, ramshackle house that was about to fall in at any moment. It would probably kill everything in it, both human and rodent, when it collapsed.

This can't be right. This place is awful. Let's get back on the trailer and go someplace that has some grass. I'll even lead the way.

Danny and Alise didn't make any moves to get me back on the trailer. I started to worry that this wasn't a joke.

"NO!" I screamed, rearing up on my hind legs, swinging my body and trying to get away. "I don't want to stay here! There's no food!"

I worked myself up into a rearing, screaming frenzy. Then suddenly, when I threw my nose in the air, snorting to clear my nostrils, I smelled something. I took in a huge gulp of air, curling my lip up in order to get the smell deeper into my nose to help figure out what the scent could be. Horses! I smelled mares! This might not be too bad after all.

Danny stroked my neck while holding on tightly to my lead rope. "Easy, boy. This is your new home."

Really? This is my new home? You're leaving me here? There might be mares here, but there's no food. Seriously, you can't leave me here.

I dropped my head down a bit, trying to see the rest of my new herd. Maybe we could all get out of here together.

"Here, Alise," Danny said as he handed my lead rope over to her. "Hold on to your new horse while I put Loco and Lazy up in the back."

"Um, okay." Alise's voice sounded higher and more nervous than before. Her hands turned white as her grip on my lead rope tightened. "Hurry, though."

"Hurry? Why, what's wrong? Are you having second thoughts now that we have him home? He'll be fine. He just needs to get used to us. I'll be right back."

Alise allowed me to graze while we waited for Danny to confine the two mares in the back. It had been so long since I had eaten real grass instead of dry, crunchy hay that I had forgotten how sweet and tasty real grass was.

A few minutes later Danny came back, carrying a bucket. It smelled like flowers. It didn't smell like food, but it was interesting nonetheless.

"Here boy." He offered me what he was carrying. "Have a snack."

I put my nose in the bucket and snorted as small brown pieces of sweet smelling dust floated around the bucket and came towards my eyes. I threw my head up and backed away. *What am I supposed to do with this?*

Danny took a handful of the mixture out and held it under my nose. "It's okay. It's just grain."

Grain? Never heard of it. It smells sweet. Is it something I'm supposed to eat? I took my lip and played with the grain in his hand. Small pieces of it dropped out of his palm.

"Don't play with it, silly boy." Alise said, sounding more relaxed, "You're supposed to eat it."

I took a few pieces of grain in my mouth. It was like nothing I had ever tasted. It was as sweet as new shoots of spring grass still covered with morning dew. It was delicious! I bobbed my head up and down, and curled my lips with excitement. If I wouldn't be able to eat fresh grass, this was definitely the next best thing.

"Have you decided on a name for him yet?" Danny asked as I was enjoying my newly found favorite food.

"Midnight. I think I'm gonna call him Midnight," Alise answered. "He's all black, so he looks like it does out here at night without any lights on. Or maybe I should call him Licorice! You know, like black licorice…."

"Nah. I think Midnight suits him better than Licorice."

I shook my head. *Midnight, Licorice, I don't care what you call me. Just let me eat. By the way, this bucket's empty.*

*****

I didn't get to eat for long before I was dragged, kicking and screaming, into the dry, grassless wasteland that was to be my new home. When I saw the mares my excitement returned, but then I got to know them.

"Wow! Aren't you a handsome little thing?" The young paint filly bounced over to greet me.

You're half right. I am handsome, but I'm not little!

"Loco! Mind your manners!" The older mare chastised. "He just got here; give him time to adjust before you start pestering him. There will be plenty of time for us to get to know him."

"But I don't want to wait, Mother! I want to talk to him now!" Loco didn't miss a step as she headed in my direction.

Her mother was finally able to stop her with a quick nip on her hindquarters. "I told you to mind your manners. Now give him a minute to get through the gate and get settled."

I could tell immediately I would never get a moment's peace and quiet again. That paint filly was quite the talker. If she thought it, she said it. By the end of the evening, I had heard all their stories at least twice, told in the quick, forward manner in which Loco does everything.

They were also mustangs. Lazy was from the wilds of Oregon. She told me she was rounded up and captured several years ago, when she was still pregnant with Loco, and went through the same auction process that had so recently brought me

57

into their herd. Loco's father was also part of the herd of mustangs from Oregon, but, for whatever reason, the humans had released him back into the wild. Loco was born in captivity, and had never known what it was like to be wild and free. Lazy still remembered what it was like to live without fences, but many years in captivity, and having to tend to Loco constantly, had taken away all of her desire to be free again. She was content to live out her days on this tiny piece of grassless wasteland in exchange for an occasional meal of grain and hay.

Oh, that reminded me.... "How often do we get to eat the food that comes in the bucket? I've never had anything like that before."

"What? The grain?" Lazy asked. "The man brings some out to us every few days."

"What about the female? How often does she feed us?"

"We don't see her much at all. But now that you're her horse, maybe she'll come out more."

"Wait a minute. 'Her horse?' I belong to somebody? No, something's wrong. I don't belong to anyone."

"That's what you think." Loco smirked. "Just wait until they make you carry them around."

"What? Carry them? I'll never carry a human on my back!" I thought of Father and the day he told me those words.

"Oh? We'll just see about that," Loco said, giggling as she walked away.

I had plenty of time to mull over Loco's words. The humans had left and didn't return until the sun was up the next day. I was so hungry I was in a pretty foul mood and feeling quite sorry for myself. Here I was, a mustang, used to running wild and free, eating and drinking whatever and whenever I wanted, now reduced to living in a small, barren dirt lot with nothing to do and nothing to eat except for some dried out hay that was kept in the back of a metal box and the promise of some of that sweet grain every few days. What had my life turned into?

Little did I know, things were about to get even worse!

*****

One morning, after I had been exploring what little there was to explore and getting used to my new home for a few days, Danny came out bright and early carrying big, heavy items in each hand.

Uh, oh!

I had seen other horses wear these things when the humans rode them. I got a sick feeling in the pit of my stomach.

"Alright, Midnight, today's the day." Danny grabbed my halter. "We're going to get you all trained up so Alise can start riding you."

As Danny started brushing my coat, I thought of Father again, and heard his voice.

I would rather die than to allow a human to get up on my back.

I panicked. I didn't want to let Father down, so I knew I had to get away. And fast. I threw my head hard up into the air, breaking the clip on the lead rope that tied me down. As soon as I heard the SNAP I ran to the other end of the pasture as fast as I could.

Danny crept towards me and spoke as slowly as he walked. "Now, Midnight, there's nothing to be scared about. I'm not going to hurt you."

You want to turn me into a beast of burden! I won't let you!

I was alert and ready for Danny now. As he came closer, I darted around him, staying just out of his grasp.

"It's okay." Danny turned around to follow me, then stopped. "I know just the thing."

He walked into the little half-fallen down building and had my full attention now. I knew what he kept in that small building: grain! I waited patiently for Danny to come back out, shaking the bucket around so I could hear one of my newest, favorite sounds.

I let him come up to me. It was worth it to get a mouthful of that tasty food. As I stuck my nose into the bucket, I heard the *CLICK, CLICK* of two more lead ropes being snapped onto my halter.

Oh, how I hate that sound!

"Not taking any more chances with you." Danny announced as he led me back to where the saddle waited. "Now, let's try this again. But this time I'll let you eat while I do it."

How bad could it be, really? If I'm given grain to eat, maybe I can try this and it won't be so bad.

I stood still and allowed Danny to finish grooming my coat, while I crunched on the grain.

"First the blanket," Danny said as he approached my left side. Before he tossed the heavy pad on my back, though, he allowed me to smell it to see what it was. It didn't smell too dangerous; it reminded me of Lazy when she's hot and sweaty. Danny moved the blanket slowly away from my nose and gently placed the blanket on my back, up over my withers.

"See, boy, it's not so bad, is it?"

I disagreed. It was awkward and quite unpleasant. It was scratchy, like when I walk under a low hanging branch and a twig sticks to me. It also had a little weight to it like when the snow would sit on my back. I stood perfectly still and didn't breathe. I waited. When I didn't feel any pain or other sensation, I exhaled and dropped my nose back down into the bucket.

"Good boy, Midnight. Now let's try the saddle." Danny held up the saddle and allowed me to sniff it as well. It also smelled like Lazy. He slowly eased the saddle on my back, talking in a gentle tone the whole time. The weight of it concerned me. I have never had anything on back except for rain and snow back home in Nevada.

"Easy, boy. It's okay." Danny continued, scratching my neck. When I realized nothing more would happen, I dropped back down and continued my snack. That's when he strapped something under my belly and tightened it, the strap holding the saddle onto my back.

Now I was scared. My head was tied and I had something strapped to my back. What else could I do? I started bucking like my life depended upon it. It might!

"Whoa, now. Easy, Midnight," Danny said. "Everything's fine."

No, it's not! Get it off me now!

Of course he didn't. He tried to calm me down until I had worn myself out with all of my bucking and screaming and just stood there, hanging my head down. Worried. Panting.

"I'm not sure what all the fuss is about, Midnight, but you're going to have to get used to it." He untied my head and led me around the dusty pen. I was too tired to fight anymore. The saddle moved around slightly with each step I took. It was one of the worst feelings I've ever had in my life.

Danny led me back to where we started and tied me up again. This time he held up a metal piece that he called a "bit" to my lips and tried to put it in my mouth. I clenched my teeth together. I already had a saddle on my back; I wasn't going to let Danny put that thing in my mouth. Then, all of a sudden, Danny surprised me by getting his thumb between my lips and rubbing my tongue.

Ugh! Human taste again! I spat. But it was enough time for Danny to get that bit in my mouth. All I wanted to do was spit it out. It was cold and bitter. But he wouldn't let me. He held it there and then clipped it to my halter. So there I was, stuck, wearing a saddle, with a bit in my mouth. I was so glad Father couldn't see me. I hung my head down in shame, experiencing the worst feeling of my life.

"Oh, come on, Midnight. You look good. You look like a real horse now!"

Hmmph! I sure don't feel like a real horse anymore.

I heard Loco laughing at me from behind the fence.

*****

The next day Danny came out and continued to torture me with the saddle and bit. The only good thing was that we all got to eat two days in a row. I fought the saddle less the second day. There didn't seem to be much point to protest anymore. When I hardly bucked or kicked at all, Danny decided it was time for him to try to ride me.

Oh, what a day that was! He had brought a friend along to help him. His friend held my reins while he mounted. I felt Danny's weight drop onto my back. I held my breath and didn't move a muscle, but soon I felt him squeeze my ribs with his legs.

My mind immediately took me back to Nevada. The only time a mustang had something on his back, squeezing his ribs, it was either a wolf or a mountain lion.

Predator! Run!

I flew across the pen. Danny didn't stay up too long, which was fine by me. But he didn't quit, either. He walked up to me, had his friend hold the reins again and swung right back into the saddle. This time he didn't squeeze my sides. He had his friend walk me slowly around the pen. After the third or fourth step, I decided I really didn't like this either. If I couldn't get him off my back by running, I'd try something different.

I went into a bucking frenzy. I kept kicking long after Danny had fallen off. He tried to ride me a few more times, each ride lasting a bit longer, but with the same results: I was up, without a rider, and Danny was down, on the ground, without a horse.

"Alright! You win. For today. I *will* ride you, though," Danny promised as he left.

It wasn't over. Danny came out the next day, and the day after that. We went through the same routine every time. He'd try to ride me, and I would try not to be ridden. By the end of the week, he was bruised and worn out, but he grew quieter every time he mounted; quieter with his voice, his hands, and his seat. And since he was settling down, little by little, I became more tolerant of having him up on my back, and didn't try to get rid of him every time.

One evening, Danny brought Alise along with him while he fed us. She asked, "When do you think I'll get to ride?"

"Ride who? Lazy or Midnight?"

"Midnight, of course. You know, *my* horse!"

"I've been working with him for a couple of days now, and I think he's ready for you. How about first thing tomorrow morning?"

Danny, you're kidding, right? I don't want you up there, much less Alise.

"Oh, Danny," Alise squealed, throwing her arms around his neck, "I can't wait!"

Oh, I can!

The next day dawned sunny and warm. Danny and Alise arrived while the grass was still wet with morning dew. I felt their excitement mixed with nervousness. Alise took her time brushing my coat and combing through my mane and tail, talking to me the entire time. "So, Midnight," she whispered to me, "I'm finally going to ride you today. Pretty soon we'll be able to go on rides with Danny and Lazy. Won't that be fun?"

Fun? Uh, no, not really. I'd rather we didn't.

I could sense through her short hard strokes that she was becoming more nervous than excited at the thought of riding me. I felt the same. When Alise had finished grooming my back Danny helped her saddle me, and I had decided to accept the bit without any disagreement.

The trouble came when Alise went to mount. Since she wasn't experienced with horses in general, much less riding one, it wasn't a good mount. I *tried* to stand as still as I could. I *tried* to remain as calm as possible as her butt slammed into the saddle, bouncing on my back. And I *tried* to be quiet as I could when she picked up the reins too quickly, gagging me with the bit. But when she jabbed her heels into my ribs, I couldn't stand it a moment longer!

I started bucking, and bucking, and bucking!

Alise started screaming, and screaming, and screaming!

She flew off of my back and landed hard. She lay quiet - for a moment.

"Danny," she screamed. "Help me, please!" She started wailing. "That's it, I'm done! I don't ever want to ride him again! I don't even like him anymore!"

"You have to understand he's wild. He's going to be a little rough around the edges. He needs more time to be trustworthy and quiet when he's ridden."

"I don't care, he almost killed me! He's more than just *rough*."

Danny sighed, untacked me and turned me back out with the two mares without saying a word.

"That was some ride you gave Alise today," Loco smirked. "I can't wait until they try to ride me again. I'm gonna do the same thing!"

The next day Danny put a large wooden sign in the yard: BLACK HORSE FOR SALE.

Although I didn't know what the sign said, I felt it in my bones it wasn't good. Turned out, though, I was wrong again.

CHAPTER 6 — KOBI

The day I met Daisy is the day that changed my life forever. It started out like every other day. Loco, Lazy and I all awoke hungry, as usual, and tried to forage on the small dirt lot for something to eat as best we could. Around midday, when it was starting to get too hot to stay out in the open and getting close to nap time, a large white truck I'd never seen before pulled into the yard. I wondered who would come to visit us and watched as two humans got out of the vehicle and came over to the fence.

The male was tall, really tall, with short dark hair. He moved with calm confidence towards the fence. He didn't rush over, but his long stride covered a lot of ground and before I knew it he was at the fence. He turned to look back at the female who was still getting out of the vehicle.

"Are you coming?"

"Yes. Now just hold your horses! Get it? We're here looking at a horse?" She giggled at her own comment.

Walking towards the fence, I saw she was considerably smaller than the male. She walked slower and appeared much more cautious. She flipped her short blonde hair out of her eyes and looked around. I could tell she lacked the confidence he had.

I was curious as to who they might be and went over to check them out. The female started pulling up grass on her side of the fence.

Oh, I hope that's for me. Yes, it is!

She came over to where I was standing and offered me the sweet grass. I was very hungry, but didn't want to scare her off, so I moved my lips gently to take the grass from her, careful not to let my teeth graze her open hand. I noticed both humans had a kindness around their eyes. Within minutes, Danny and Alise arrived too and the introductions began, distracting the new human and ending my snack.

"Hi! I'm Daisy and this is my boyfriend, Rex. He talked to you about the black horse you have for sale."

"Yeah, come on in and take a closer look." Danny said, opening the gate to our pasture. "He seems to like you already."

I suspected that this human, Daisy, was my chance to get out of here, and finally fill my empty stomach, so I poured on the charm. I went over to her and rubbed my head on her shoulder. I sucked on her fingers, but was careful not to bite.

My heart sank when she said, "He's very sweet, but is he rideable?"

Here we go again. What is it with humans wanting to ride horses?

"Of course he is," Danny replied. "Would you like to ride him?"

What? Come on, Danny. Me, ride? You know me better than that. Don't you? You remember what happened last time with Alise.

"No, not yet. I would like to see *you* ride him. I want to see how he moves."

I was as good as gold. I figured if Daisy bought me and I got out of here, maybe I would have more food and wouldn't be hungry all the time. She and I could work out any riding issues later.

Daisy helped groom me. She had nice firm brush strokes, reaching all of my itchy places. I liked that. It made me think she was much more comfortable around horses than other humans. She stood back and watched my reactions as Danny saddled and bridled me. Not waiting to be directed, she stepped right up and held my head as Danny mounted. I caught my breath, hoping

Danny wouldn't ask me to do something I didn't know how to do yet.

Daisy backed away slowly and stood next to Rex, whispering to him about me. "Watch his legs and his head while he walks. See if he has any jerky movements that might indicate lameness."

Jerky movements? Me? Why I've never been lame a day in my life.

I put on a show for them. I didn't bolt or buck the entire time. I walked along slowly and allowed Danny to steer me around the pen. I knew I had passed the test when I heard Daisy say, "Okay, he looks great and he's sweet, but I need to bring a friend by to see him before I can buy him. I'll be boarding him at her house and need her approval first. Will that be okay?"

Would that be okay? That would be great! I'm ready to get out of here.

Before Danny had time to answer, I saw Loco sneaking up on Rex. I wasn't sure what she was up to, but with her, well, it's never good. I looked at Rex and whinnied. *Look out, Rex!*

He spun around just in time to see Loco rearing up, aiming to land a hoof on his hip. Rex pulled back, narrowly missing her sharp hooves and a broken hip.

"Did you see that? He just warned me. That's amazing! I don't know much about horses, but I think this one's brilliant. He just saved me a trip to the emergency room."

Daisy walked over and started scratching my forehead. "What a good boy. I think Rex is right, you are brilliant! We just need Lilith to see it too."

Danny agreed for Daisy's friend, Lilith, to come over and give her seal of approval for the sale.

One down, only one more to go! I just know I can convince Lilith to adore me too.

*****

When Daisy brought Lilith out to meet me, I tried to be as charming as I could. I found it wasn't as easy as I thought. While Daisy adored me and rubbed my neck or scratched my ears any chance she got, Lilith would not come close and never once tried to touch me. She was different from Alise or Daisy in almost every way. Lilith was a tall, thin, older woman. She didn't seem to have any soft spots on her at all; she was all harsh lines and sharp corners. Even the way she wore her hair, tightly pulled back in a ponytail, without a single gray hair loose, made me think Lilith was a severe, strict woman.

Her words were clipped short, like she didn't have time to talk to anyone. When she did speak, she had a certain tone about her; the words themselves didn't seem bad, but the way she said them let whoever she was speaking to know Lilith thought she was smarter and better than they were. I never saw her lips curl into a smile. Why was Daisy friends with her? More importantly, how could I convince her to let Daisy take me away from this barren dry lot?

"Well, Lilith, what do you think?" There was a nervous catch in Daisy's voice.

"It's hard to tell since he hasn't been tested for Equine Anemia. Get a vet out here to make sure he's healthy. As long as his Coggins test comes back negative and he won't infect my horses with anything, I'll let you board him at my house."

*****

I passed the vet's exam with flying colors, and the day to go to my new home had arrived. Daisy, excited to be my new human, came early to get me. Lilith came with her to oversee everything and ensure there wouldn't be any problems. While I hoped there wouldn't be any problems either, I wish Rex would have come instead; he seemed much calmer, which seemed to rub off on Daisy.

Their plan was to walk me the three miles back to Lilith's house, which is where Daisy would be keeping me since she didn't have a barn or pasture to call her own. I walked up to the fence so Daisy could scratch my forehead and rub my neck and shoulders until it was time for us to leave.

"I hope you enjoy Midnight and that he works out for you," Danny said as he looked for my halter and lead rope.

"Thanks, I know he will," Daisy continued to scratch my ear and smile as she moved her hand down to rub my forehead.. "And we've changed his name. He's no longer Midnight. We're going to call him Kobi."

"Kobi. That's, um, an, um, interesting name," Alise said.

"Rex and I figured that a unique horse, like Kobi, needed a unique name. Since he's a mustang from out west, we started looking at Indian names. The Comanche Indians had a word for horse, which I can't pronounce, and a different word for wild horses: Kobi. I think Kobi is a perfect fit for him."

I couldn't agree more; a unique name for a unique horse! I think I'm going to like my new human and my new name. Kobi.

After what seemed an eternity, it was finally time for us to walk to my new home. At times the walk was frightening. Large trucks thundered by and humans blew the horns of their vehicles, like they had never seen a horse walking down the road before, but Danny had planned for this. He knew of my love for grain, so the last thing he handed Daisy before turning over my lead rope was a bucket full of yummy sweet grain. Every time I started to get a little excited, Daisy offered me the bucket of food. It was great. I ate the entire way to my new home and gave no more thoughts to Loco, Lazy, Danny, Alise, or the wasteland I came from.

When we got to my new home, the first thing I noticed was that my new pasture was wonderful—it had grass! I had the entire, luscious, grass-filled field all to myself, too.

Daisy whispered as she turned me loose in the pasture to eat and explore, "Kobi, I may not be the smartest human you'll ever meet, but I promise you no one will ever love you more than I do. I will always do my best to take care of you."

Slipping my nose out of my halter, I turned to look at her. *Daisy, you've already shown me more love by bringing me to a place with food. A full belly means a lot to me. Don't worry; I will always try to do my best to take care of you too!*

Before I took off to explore my new grass-filled pasture, I spotted two other horses, both mares, in a pasture next to mine. The mares ran to the gate to meet me. I wandered over and touched noses with them to be polite, but before they had a chance to talk, I wandered to the farthest part of the pasture, as far from them as the fence would let me go. With the memory of

Loco and Lazy still fresh in my mind, I didn't know if I wanted to get involved with any more crazy mares just yet.

I didn't have much choice, though. After stuffing myself for a week on all the grass I could eat, I was sent into the pasture with the mares. The pasture I left was closed off and we were restricted from it. It wouldn't have been too bad except it was the only pasture that had any grass. My new pasture didn't have a single blade. It was awful. I was hungry all the time again. The one thing that made it even worse was I could see my former pasture and all that tantalizing, luscious green grass and smell its sweet juiciness, but I just couldn't reach it. I was living a food-restricted nightmare.

My first day with the mares was stressful, with both me and the younger mare, Malevolent, trying to establish our dominance over the herd. The older mare, Brownie, didn't argue one bit about the leadership. "I'm too old for this nonsense," she muttered as she wandered away, "Leadership is for the young."

Malevolent , though, was another story. She saw my arrival as an opportunity to be the leader she always wanted to be. Malevolent was named for her personality flaws. She was a spoiled brat. The name fit her to a tee. It didn't matter what I said or did, she always had some smart remark or rude comeback. She had a quick temper and didn't mind unleashing her quick tongue or a swift kick or nip. She could take it as well as she could dish it! When all was said and done, though, I found I spent less time with docile and easy going Brownie, and more time with Malevolent, because I understood her better. She was more like the feisty wild horses I had grown up with.

She did have one habit I just couldn't understand no matter how hard I tried. Every night when we were given hay, she would run around to at least one pile and pee on it.

"What are you doing?" I asked the first time I saw her squat over a pile of hay.

"Keeping you and Brownie from eating my hay."

"You're right about that. Why do you pee on it though, instead of just trying to run us off, or even share the hay?"

"If you must know, I'd rather spend my time eating my hay instead of running around for it. As for sharing, it's never been something I enjoy doing. Now that neither one of you want it, this hay is all mine."

"That's not only hateful, it's the most disgusting and disturbing thing I've ever seen. Peeing on your food. It's just wrong."

"It might be wrong, but it's all mine."

From that point on, I always tried to be the first horse out to the hay after dinner. It saved me from having to sniff each pile of hay first. Some nights, I would have to eat my hay listening to

Malevolent chuckling to herself and making me wonder if she had gotten to that pile first and peed on it just to be mean.

*****

I knew the day was coming when Daisy would want to ride. Surprising both of us, our first ride together was uneventful. I think we both were expecting the worst, but Daisy just talked calmly to me the entire time she was grooming me. Before I knew what was going on, she had me saddled and was ready to place the bit in my mouth. I even took it from her hand without a fuss. Daisy had her mother, Holly, hold me while she placed her foot into the stirrup.

I behaved well for Holly, too. She looked exactly like Daisy, just a little older. While she stood there, I didn't move a muscle. I tried not to breathe. Daisy took the reins in her hands, squeezed my sides with her legs, and commanded, "Walk."

I did as she asked. I walked. When she told me to "Whoa," I again did as she asked, and I stopped. Our first ride together only lasted about ten minutes, but I dripped with sweat. I was so nervous; I was afraid to do the wrong thing or make a slight misstep. I liked my new home and my new human, and I wanted to keep both.

The ride went perfectly. It was actually easy. We were starting to build our relationship together, based on trust. I had to trust her not to hurt me, and she had to trust my instincts and realize that sometimes I knew more than I was letting her know. So far we trusted and liked each other. It was a good place to start.

I tried to keep Daisy safe, like I promised her, but sometimes she didn't catch on. During one of our rides, we were working on walking and stopping, and then continuing again. Nothing exciting, to be sure, but I realized it was going to be the baseline for our communication together. Well, Daisy didn't realize at the time, and neither did I, but we had stopped too close to a fence, and her toes were resting inside the wire hole when we stopped. She gave me the cue to walk forward and her foot grazed along the inside of the wire, creating a terrifying sound, like we were being attacked by something right beside us. My instincts took over. Danger! I didn't hesitate. I took off running - fast!

Hold on, Daisy, I'll save us! I'll get us out of here!

I thought we were running for our lives. We came to the tight corner in the pasture. There was a low hanging tree to the left and another fence topped with barbed wire to our right. Scary, but I knew we could make it. If she could just hold on, I would bring her to safety.

She jumped off! I couldn't believe it. One moment Daisy was up there, holding on. The next moment she was down, rolling around in the sand. What was she thinking? I had everything under control! And she jumped off! Stupid as that move was, I couldn't just leave her laying there. She might need me to protect her from the danger we just ran from. I turned around to go check on her.

When I got there, Daisy wasn't stirring. Her chest was moving up and down, so I knew she was still breathing. I walked up and nudged her with my nose, urging her to get up.

Are you okay? I told you to hold on.

With her eyes still closed, she reached up and scratched my forehead. "Oh, Kobi," she whispered, "you came back for me." She rolled over to her side and slowly pushed herself up. "You are such a good boy."

She leaned into my neck and gave me a kiss.

That special moment was interrupted when Lilith sprinted over, screeching, "What happened? What did Kobi do to you?"

Daisy didn't have her breath back all the way and was leaning on me for support. "My foot got caught in the fence when we stopped, so when we started again it rattled along the fence and spooked him."

"You know you have to get right back up on him, don't you?" Lilith snarled. "Here, I'll even hold him for you."

Daisy mounted, oh so slowly. I could tell she was hurting from the fall and had already gotten stiff in just that short period of time. I felt terrible for her, but I had no way to make her understand, all she had needed to do was to trust me and hold on. I would've taken care of the rest.

That was the first time I realized humans would punish me for doing something they didn't like, but it wasn't Daisy. She wasn't the punishing type. She preferred our relationship to be based on trust and respect. But Lilith? Oh, Lilith was definitely the punishing type.

That night, after Daisy jumped off, was the first of many nights Lilith deliberately left me out of the feeding rotation. At first, I thought she had forgotten, so I ran around whinnying and nickering to remind her.

"None for you tonight, Kobi. You threw your rider. Bad horses don't get grain." She flung my hay into the dirt.

I soon found out there were other punishable offenses: chasing Brownie off of her food, playing too rough with Malevolent, playing with any of the other animals, or playing at all with Brownie. With these new rules in place, I was bored, often bad tempered, and usually very hungry.

*****

81

A few weeks later, Daisy and I were working in the front field. She wanted me to go into the front corner, but every time we headed in that direction I would get a feeling of dread in the pit of my stomach. Then I realized why. It smelled. Really bad. Like something had died. The air even felt different in that part of the field, almost electrified. Daisy must not have noticed the horrific smell or the change in the air since she was bound and determined to make me walk through that stench. I was just as determined not to. Every time we got close to that spot, I would throw myself into reverse, backing up until I felt we were a safe distance away. Daisy didn't understand why.

I didn't want to ride there, but she kept digging her heels into my side to try and convince me to. The harder she dug, the more I backed up. When I could sense her frustration was peaking, she dismounted. Then she led me into the stinking spot and we stopped. She put her foot in the stirrup, ready to mount. I stayed put for a second. Then I felt her put all her weight in the stirrup and swing her leg across my back. That was enough. No more Mister Nice Mustang.

Jigging and tossing my head around, I squealed. *No! I don't want to be here! Don't you get it?*

I took off running to the other side of the field, where the horrible stench couldn't reach my nose. That was the second time I found myself without Daisy on my back! This time I didn't go back for her. If she was foolish enough to make me ride through the disgusting odor, she could just lie there. I was hungry and frustrated. I needed to teach her to trust my instincts sometimes. Since I was a safe distance away, I began to graze.

A few moments later, Daisy was back on her feet and moving slow. She seemed to be gasping for breath, and it wasn't coming back to her as quickly as the last time. She stumbled up to me, grabbed my reins and grunted rather firmly, "Let's go, Kobi." She led me back to the barn, where she remounted, safely away from all of the terrible smells of the front field, and we rode around the barn for a while.

Okay, I knew I had been a little harsh with Daisy, running away like that and not going back for her. It probably wasn't one of the best ways to try to protect her, but I didn't know how else to let her know we were in a really bad place up there. Even though it was difficult for her to understand, maybe next time she would trust me. Daisy needed a little tough love.

*****

I had spooked Daisy more than I thought by tossing her. Our rides alone together stopped. The only time Daisy would climb on my back was if she had someone close by to help her. That was usually Rex or Holly. It made me sad; I had enjoyed our quiet rides together.

One day Daisy and Holly came out to the pasture and caught both me and Malevolent.

This is going to be interesting. I wonder what they have in mind for today. Why do they want Malevolent?

I became even more suspicious when I noticed Daisy was tacking up Malevolent, and Holly was preparing to tack me up.

What's going on? You're confused, Holly. I'm Daisy's horse. Go ride Malevolent.

"Looks like you're getting a new rider today, Kobi." Malevolent smirked. Then she snorted, "This oughta be good!"

I didn't say another word, just tried to remain calm.

Why doesn't Daisy want to ride me? Maybe I shouldn't have run away the last time we were together. I knew I was a much better horse than Malevolent. I didn't want a different rider up on me. This is so unfair! *I want my Daisy.*

Holly and I followed Daisy and Malevolent to the front field. When we got there, I stood still, as I had been taught, waiting to be mounted. Holly got up. We waited for Daisy to get up on Malevolent. It took a while because Malevolent had no ground manners. Even though Daisy had also been working with Malevolent, the horse stayed true to her bratty name, and kept jigging about. Finally, she quit playing her silly little games and stood still. Daisy mounted.

Now, I didn't like this. Not one bit. I had a strange rider on my back and Daisy was up on another horse. We started walking. It didn't feel right to me.

What are you doing up there? You're not supposed to be up there! I'm Daisy's horse! Only Daisy can be up there! Get off!

I started to rebel in the only way I knew how: bucking. I screamed and ended every scream with a solid buck. Holly stayed on. So I added a rear to my buck. First I'd go up on my front legs into a buck and then rock back on my hind legs into a rear. I had seen other mustangs try this rear/buck when people tried to mount them at the holding facilities, but I had never tried the combination myself. Very effective!

"No! Kobi, No!" Holly cried.

That was all Holly had time to say before she lost her balance and toppled off over my side. I looked back over my shoulder and saw her lying on the ground, flat on her back. Daisy spun Malevolent around, leapt off her back and sprinted over to check on her mother.

"Mom!" I heard the alarm in her voice. "Are you alright?"

Uh, oh. Did I go too far again?

I got what I wanted. Holly was off my back and Daisy was off of Malevolent. Why, then, did I feel as if I had done a terrible thing?

"You've done it now, Kobi." Malevolent sneered. "I wouldn't be surprised if she sold you."

"What do you mean?" I asked, frightened and instantly regretting my decision to buck.

"You've dumped your last two riders. No one wants you now. Your days are numbered out here, Kobi. Goodbye and good riddance." Malevolent was gloating.

Uh-oh! That's why I have that sick feeling in my stomach. I thought maybe I had pushed them too far, and I might be right.

"What do I do now? I don't want to be sold again."

"If I were you, I'd be as nice and docile as I could from here on out. Still, it's probably too late."

I vowed right then and there I would never throw my rider off my back again, no matter who they were.

Daisy helped her mother sit up. "Let me go put the horses up and then I'll come back for you. Okay?"

"Leave Kobi here," Holly said. "Hook his reins over the saddle horn so he can't graze while you're gone. Then when you get back over here, you can help me get back up on him."

What is this stupid rule humans have about getting back on after they fall off? Are they trying to prove something to me or to themselves?

Daisy came over and looped my reins over the saddle horn. "Bad boy," she scolded. "I can't believe you did that. I'm so disappointed in you, Kobi."

Malevolent was right. Daisy was mad at me. I know she promised to always love me, but I had hurt her and let her down. She was going to sell me now, I just knew it. I hung my head in shame.

I'm so sorry. It won't happen again, I promise. Please, please give me another chance.

But Daisy just turned her back on me as she led Malevolent back to the barn to get untacked. Malevolent kept laughing at me until she got so far away that I couldn't hear her anymore.

I walked over to Holly and tried to nuzzle her up to her feet. *Come on, get up. I wanted Daisy to ride me, but I didn't want you to get hurt. Get up.*

"You were a very bad boy," she told me. "You can't keep doing that, Kobi."

*****

After that episode I tried hard to be as agreeable as I could. But something was different; Daisy's trust in me was shattered. Not only would she not ride me when she was by herself, but now there always had to be a person on the ground to walk beside me while she rode. Since she didn't feel she could trust me anymore to behave myself, spook, run away, get angry, or start bucking, the other person would use a lead rope attached to my halter just to make sure I didn't act up. It was humiliating. Based on my bad behavior and poor judgment, though, I guess I deserved it.

Every time I saw a new human come to the barn, either with Lilith or Daisy, Malevolent would run up to me, sneering, with her head high. "This is it. You're on your way out now."

I didn't believe her. I couldn't believe her. I never saw a big sign in the yard like I did at my old house with Danny and Alise. Daisy wouldn't give up on me now, would she? She still came out and spent time with me. I felt it down in my bones, she still believed in her heart of hearts she would be able to train me into becoming her partner. First she had to believe in me again. I worked as hard as I could to show her all of my potential. I wanted to regain her trust.

One day I overheard Lilith and Daisy deep in discussion. Daisy's eyes looked sad, and her color wasn't good; she was as pale as the sand in the barren pasture. I wandered over to her, wondering what hateful, untrue things Lilith was telling her about me now.

"Either you sell him or send him to a trainer," Lilith snapped. "You're not progressing with Kobi the way you should be."

"I'm doing the best I can."

"I know." Lillith patted Daisy's hand. "I just hate to see you put in so much effort and still not get anywhere with him."

"I'm not going to sell him and I don't want to send him away to a trainer, either. I don't know what trainers would do with him when I'm not around. Besides, why would I want a trainer to train Kobi and then not train me to work with him? I don't want Kobi to be able to do all of these amazing things with someone else, just to have the same issues with me when I ride him again."

"Then get a trainer to come out here. But you need to quit talking about it and do something. Either get him trained or get him out of here." Lilith turned on her heel and stomped away.

"Oh, Kobi." Daisy wrapped her arms around my neck and started to cry into my mane. "Maybe Lilith's right. We do need help."

If that's the case then it's the first time Lilith's been right about anything since I got here.

CHAPTER 7 — TRAINING BEGINS

Daisy had been walking on eggshells for weeks now, jumping at every little sound and trembling whenever she rode. She appeared even less sure of herself than when we first met. Her visits had become less and less frequent and she seemed to come out only when Lilith was not around. She seemed anxious. I knew something was up.

"All the signs are there, Kobi, I'm only surprised you haven't figured it out sooner," Malevolent taunted me one afternoon. "I told you Daisy is getting rid of you."

I refused to believe that. I heard Daisy say she wasn't going to sell me. Did she change her mind? I thought Daisy and I were determined to make this partnership work. She wouldn't be selling me now, would she? Every time she visited, I was as charming as I could be. I liked Daisy and didn't want her to sell me.

One evening as I was standing beside Daisy, afraid she would be leaving soon and never come back, I heard her take in a deep breath as Lilith approached.

"Lilith," she started quickly, "I've decided that you're right." Daisy was holding her breath, planning what to say next.

What? What was Lilith right about? Finding a trainer or selling me? I can't take this anymore! I have to know!

"Kobi and I need a trainer." The words were rushing out of Daisy now like a river. I don't think she could have stopped talking if she had to. I could sense the nervousness and anxiety pouring out of her as she spoke. "I've found a trainer I like. Her name is Wendy. I'll have to take Kobi over to her barn. Wendy will train me to do all of the work with Kobi myself. That way I'll be the one training him, under her direction. I'm moving Kobi on Sunday."

Wow! She said all of that in one breath! Wait a minute. We're moving out of here? On Sunday? To a new barn? With Wendy? What if I don't like her?

Lilith responded smugly, "Really? And how long will Kobi be gone? You may not know this, but it will be difficult to reintroduce him to my herd if he's gone too long."

"Um," Daisy swallowed, I could tell she was fearful of the direction this conversation was taking. "We won't be coming back here, Lilith. Kobi will stay with Wendy at her barn until I can buy my own property and have him live there with me and Rex."

What? We're finally leaving? And not coming back?

I quit listening. My mind was spinning. I couldn't believe it! We were going to a trainer that could help us become a better team. Then I'd get to live with Daisy all the time! No more abuse from the hands of Lilith! No more being tormented from the sassy mouth of Malevolent. No more looking at a pasture full of grass across the way while my stomach rumbled from being hungry.

Hooray! Daisy was going to take me out of here. From that point on she was no longer just my owner and my rider, she was my partner now, and the one who I knew would take care of me! She was keeping her promise. And I knew I would keep mine, too.

*****

I could hardly contain myself until Sunday. Moving Day! I didn't know what this new barn had in store for me, but I figured it had to be better than where I was. I walked onto the small red trailer the first time Daisy led me up to it. There was grain and hay in there waiting for me, so I got to eat *and* get out of here. It was going to be a great day!

Rex was in charge of driving me over to the new barn. Daisy and Holly followed along to make sure everything was going to go smoothly. I kept turning around just to make sure they were still behind us. And there they stayed, right behind us as Rex crawled down the street, making sure I wouldn't be bouncing around too much.

Finally, the trailer came to a stop and so did the truck's rumbling. Daisy jumped out and was already opening up the window by my head, clipping my lead rope into place so I could see my new home. I backed out slowly, taking in the new sights and smells. I couldn't believe it. There was grass everywhere. There were horses everywhere. Already, this place was so much better than living with Lilith, Malevolent, and Brownie. I nuzzled Daisy to say *thank you* and dropped my head to munch the sweet, sweet grass.

Our new trainer, Wendy, came out to greet Daisy and to meet me. "I have his stall all ready for him."

Stall? A stall of my own? I don't have to worry about some mare peeing on my hay anymore? This place is fantastic.

I didn't stay excited about my own stall for long though. I stayed inside 24 hours a day for the first few days, so that Wendy could be sure I was eating and drinking like I should, and not being run off of my food by others. Like I'd let that happen! By the time I finally was released from the prison, I was so frustrated I took it out on the horses who were in the pasture with me. I chased them all over the place, nipping at them if they didn't move fast enough, and kicking at them if they got in my way. It felt so good to be a dominant mustang again. I had so much fun.

However, Wendy wasn't impressed at all. She told me that if I couldn't be nice to the other horses, then I wouldn't get to play with them anymore.

To be honest, I didn't think she was serious, but I quickly found out that she was. I was confined to my stall again for bad behavior. I could only go out at night, when all of the other horses came inside. It was boring staring at the same four walls all day long. The only things that kept me from getting cabin fever was watching all the comings and goings at the barn and Daisy's visits twice a day to ride.

Each time Daisy would pull up to the barn, we would play a game. She would call my name, "Kobi. Oh, Kobi," and I would nicker to her in response. Then she would ask, "What do you want?"

I would always yell back to her, "Let me out of here!" and she would. We had so much fun together. Every time I saw her I realized how much more I looked forward to her visits and the time we were able to spend together. I was so glad we found each other.

One afternoon, after a particularly intense workout, I was dripping with sweat when Daisy untacked me.

I heard one of the barn girls, Ruth, holler, "Do you need some help getting him on the wash rack?"

"Yes, please. That would be great. He's so stubborn when it comes to hosing him down."

Stubborn? Ha! That's putting it mildly. You know how I hate that thing. You know how much I hate getting wet. Just let me roll around in the dirt. I'll be fine.

"Lead him out to the rack and I'll follow behind with the dressage whip, just to encourage him," said Ruth.

Another one of the younger barn girls, Bianca, came bounding out behind us with her whip. "I wanna help too!"

"Alright," Ruth said. "But if you come out, you have to stay in the back with me."

"Okay." Bianca's short, red curls bounced up and down as she nodded. "This is gonna be fun."

"One more thing. After we get him hooked up, your job is to keep him from trying to back off of the wash rack. I'm sure Daisy doesn't want him to flip over and hurt himself."

No worries. I don't want to flip over and hurt myself, either. Can't we just forget about this whole wash rack thing? I'd rather go back into my lonely stall than the wash rack.

Bianca only needed to hear that she could come and help too. They took me out and convinced me to get on the wash rack with the help of some cookies and by waving their whips as if they were going to pop my rump. When I finished eating all the cookies they clipped me to the cross-ties. Any time I moved, even if it were to just switch feet to find a more comfortable position, Bianca popped me in the rump for moving. She never popped me hard enough to hurt, but it sure was annoying. It didn't even matter how much Daisy or Ruth yelled at Bianca to stop hitting me and told her I wasn't trying to back up. The only response they got from Bianca was a small "Sorry." As soon as I'd shift my weight again, though, *POP*! Next came, "Sorry." *POP*! "Sorry." If it wasn't my rump that was getting whacked, it would have been comical: *POP*! Sorry. She reminded me of a young filly trying hard to please, but more trouble than she was worth—especially to my rump!

*****

After I became adjusted to Wendy's barn and my new surroundings, my training with Daisy began in earnest. Wendy always watched, and she always knew when we did things wrong. She even knew when we were doing things wrong I didn't know were wrong!

Daisy came out twice a day to work me. In the morning Wendy had Daisy and me work in the round pen, improving our communication and making sure our signals meant the same thing.: like when she would pull back on the reins and quit riding, it meant for me to stop moving forward. Or when I didn't feel like moving forward, she would spin me in a circle and show me how much easier it was to move forward in a straight line than in a circle where my nose touched her knees. That was our basic foundation for communication.

During the heat of the day I stayed in my stall. Daisy would come back in the evening, taking me into the arena to practice what we had been taught that morning. It was the hardest I'd ever worked in my life, but it was also the only escape from my boring stall. I liked having something to do with my mind and my body, and I especially liked spending my time with Daisy.

I learned a lot of other stuff in those early days, too. I learned that humans like to make sure you can't escape when you're being groomed and tacked up, so they created what they called a 'cross-tie.' A cross-tie is a lead rope clipped to each side of the halter. I couldn't go forward, backward or even move side-to-side when hooked up. I did figure out, though, that while my head was immobile, my rump was not. I would move my back end all over the place, much to Wendy's dismay. It was so much fun to annoy her, so I made sure to do it whenever I heard her coming.

By annoying Wendy, I learned about a dressage whip. It enables the humans to have a longer reach than they would with only their arms. They can stand in one spot, away from horse's moving legs, and still reach us. Wendy would just tap me on my shoulders to get my attention to stop moving on the cross-ties. I would let her think it worked until she put the whip down, then I would move again. She was so much fun to play with.

I also found out humans love to spray stuff on their horses. Now, back in Nevada, I wasn't fond of getting caught in a snowstorm or even a rainstorm. I don't like to feel anything wet seeping into my coat or onto my skin. We had a few bugs out there, but there are tons more bugs in Florida. Oh, and the gnats. Did I mention I'm allergic to them? And they are everywhere! And it seemed that wherever those little beasties landed on me, I would have an itchy spot for days. It didn't matter to me if I scratched all of my hair off in the process; I just had to scratch those itches.

When Daisy saw my torment with the gnats and biting flies she decided it would be a good idea to spray fly spray all over my coat. Now, I would rather scratch my own skin off than to allow her to spray that acid on me. Not that it hurt; it just annoyed every fiber in my being to be wet at all! Daisy wasn't about to give up and let the bugs win, so she walked into my stall, sprayed everything like a mad woman, chased me into a corner so I couldn't move away, and finally coated me with that smelly, nasty spray. While I'll never admit it to her, that spray did keep some of the biting flies at bay, so eventually I would just stand there and allow her to spray me. All the while I gave her the stink-eye.

The other thing I learned in those early days was that when my stomach hurt, I didn't want to do anything. One day right after our morning workout, I started to feel a twinge in my stomach. It wasn't especially painful, but something wasn't agreeing with me. The feeling kept getting more and more intense as Daisy untacked me. I didn't even put up a fight when she led me to the wash rack. Maybe, just maybe, cooling down would make my stomach feel better. It didn't.

Daisy was in a bit of a tizzy that morning too. Her nieces were visiting her and this was their last day in town and she wanted to spend more time with them. She was trying to get all of her barn chores done as quickly as she could, so she didn't notice I wasn't grazing, she just turned me out to pasture. Before she walked too far away, the pain in my stomach became so severe that I dropped to the ground. I started biting at my stomach to see if I could remove whatever was hurting me. When that didn't work, I tried to roll around on my back, hoping to dislodge what was causing the pain. That didn't work either. By now, I had Daisy's full attention.

She sprinted back into the barn and grabbed my halter. Then she ran back out to where I was laying down in the pasture and slipped the halter over my nose. I had never seen Daisy run anywhere before, so I knew that whatever was bothering me, it must be serious.

"Come on, Kobi," she whispered with concern and more than a little fear in her voice. "We've got to get you up, boy. Then I have to go find Wendy. She'll know what to do."

Daisy kept gently coaxing me until I was up on my feet, but I didn't feel like standing up. My stomach hurt too bad to do anything, so I kept trying to lie back down. At this point, Daisy was yelling for help. I didn't want to move anymore. The sun was beating down on my dark coat. Sweat formed all over my body. I didn't even care how hot I was because I just wanted the pain to stop. Wendy heard Daisy's cries for help, and as soon as she saw me struggling to stay upright she grabbed the closest dressage whip and came running to the field.

"I think he's trying to colic." Tears spilled down Daisy's face. "He has all of the symptoms: trying to lie down, rolling, and biting his belly."

I wasn't sure if I was trying to colic or not, but boy, my stomach was killing me.

"Don't you get all weepy on me now," Wendy chastised. "This isn't the time to panic. Trust me, Daisy; I'll let you know when it's time for you to panic. This isn't it. Now get him up! Start leading him to the barn. I'll encourage him to keep moving from behind."

Wendy really knew how to take charge of the situation. As soon as they got me in a dark stall, they turned the fan on to help cool me down. Wendy stuck something very sharp into my neck; I barely registered it pricking my skin, my mind was only on my stomachache.

"This is banamine," she explained to Daisy. "It'll kick in within the next 20 minutes. It's just a pain reliever, kinda like aspirin for humans. These young horses can't stand any type of discomfort, so they make a big deal about everything.

"In about 20 minutes, mix him up some bran mash and mineral oil and see if he'll eat it. If he does, take him out to the round pen and lunge him for awhile. He needs to stay in motion to get his belly moving things around again. He may not feel like it, but it's your job to make sure that he moves. Then offer him some more mash. But don't give him any hay at all. Hay can get caught in his gut and keep the mash from passing, doing more harm than good. He can have all the grass he wants.

"Keep this up all day and don't worry. Kobi is going to be just fine; I'd tell you if he's not. Now stop crying!"

Wendy was right. Before long the pain went away and I was able to function like a mustang again. I devoured all of the bran mashes but hated all of the lunging. Daisy never did make it to say goodbye to her nieces that day. She stayed with me the entire time and prepared me snacks every little while before making me work out all of the gas that created my stomachache in the first place. I'm glad she stayed with me. I don't know if I could have survived the day without her by my side.

By that night I had made a full recovery. I still wasn't allowed hay or solid food for another day, but it was okay. If I never experience colic again, it will be fine by me.

Once Daisy felt sure my stomach was better, we resumed our intense training schedule.

One evening I was put out to pasture early before Daisy made her evening trek out to visit. When she came into the pasture with my halter, I saw something chasing her. Out of the corner of my eye, I saw a coyote running up right behind Daisy.

Daisy, look out! Coyote! Behind you! Watch out! You're in danger!

I had to protect Daisy. I ran to position myself between her and the dangerous coyote. It didn't back down from me or run away. I tried to chase it down to keep it away from her, kicking out at the offensive beast.

"Kobi, no! Whoa! Stop!" Daisy yelled at me, waving her arms to get my attention. "That's just Cuzzin. He's my dog. He's not going to hurt you." Daisy ran up and stood between me and the dog, scratching his ears. "You'll just have to get used to him. You don't have to worry about him. He's not dangerous, but he's not that bright."

What? Let me get this straight. You have a predator. A dog...and a stupid dog, at that. He gets to go home with you every night while I have to stay here? This really doesn't seem fair. I don't trust that dog. I'll be keeping my eye on him, making sure you're safe and that dog doesn't do anything stupid.

Daisy brought that dumb dog, Cuzzin, out with her a couple more times. Each time I would find Cuzzin alone, I would corner him, letting him know I didn't like him. Not one bit. Once I chased that dumb dog all the way across the field and Cuzzin had to run into the barn for protection. I think Daisy got the hint after that. She stopped bringing him out. I didn't miss him at all.

After all of the our intense training, the excitement of my colic, and the drama with Cuzzin, the rest of the summer passed in a blur of more riding, baths on the wash rack, trying to avoid the fly spray, and scratching all of those bug bites. When the days turned cooler and the nights became longer, it was time for Daisy to go back to school and our visits were cut back to just evenings and weekends.

CHAPTER 8 — BIG JAKE

I will never forget the following winter. That's when Big Jake entered my life. Most humans had no idea what kind of beast he was: horse, mule, or maybe even a buffalo. Rex didn't help matters much either. He kept telling everyone Jake was a Muffalo: part mustang, part buffalo. The funny thing was that most people didn't even question it. They actually believed him.

In their defense, Jake *was* a strange looking creature. To start with, he was massive. The top of my back only came up to his shoulder, and I would have to stretch my neck to its limit to rest my head on his back. Not that I had any intentions of doing it!

To complete his colossal appearance, Jake was the thickest animal I ever saw. A single one of Jake's legs was as wide as two of mine put together. You couldn't see a single rib on him, and when you saw him from the back, his rump looked like the largest, most perfect giant apple. Adding to his bulk was his hair. He was the hairiest creature I had ever laid eyes on. Jake's hair was so thick it curled all over his body. He even had a full beard under his chin, not to mention a moustache that curled from his lips. Jake smelled like a horse, acted like a horse, but he absolutely, positively did not look like a horse!

"What are you?" I asked him when we were out to pasture together, about a week after he joined the herd.

"Horse," Jake mumbled through mouthfuls of hay, not even bothering to lift his head up. "What do you think I am?"

"I know you're a horse," I said, getting frustrated with this apparent dimwit, "but you sure don't look like any horse that I've ever seen."

"Oh, have you seen everything, then?" Jake's mouth was still full of hay. He still hadn't looked up at me.

"Well, no, but I've seen you, and you sure do look odd."

"It's the donkeys; they ate my tail." He grabbed another bite of hay before he turned his ample hindquarters toward me to show me his half-eaten tail. "They ate everything. And I do mean everything."

"It's not just your tail. Why do you have all that long hair?" I had never seen another horse with a coat that thick and shaggy. "Is something wrong with you?"

"Oh, all of this?" Jake bit at the hair on his side. "All of the horses back in Kentucky have this much hair. Especially all the other work horses."

"What do you mean 'work horses'?"

"I was a work horse. Back in Kentucky, I pulled logs out of the woods. Humans would put a really tight work collar around my neck." Jake pointed out where he had a gash above the withers on his neck almost as deep as one of my hooves, where a collar had bitten into his skin. "Then they would tie me to the trees they had cut down. As soon as the tree was all hooked up to my collar, they made me pull them out. If we horses didn't move fast enough, we would get whipped for our troubles."

"I bet you got whipped a lot then," I laughed. "The only thing you look like you can do quickly is eat!"

"I did." Jake whispered, "I did." I could tell he didn't want to talk about it anymore because he plodded off to the other end of the pasture, leaving me alone to finish the rest of the hay. Without Jake around, it left me to my thoughts. How could humans be so cruel? I've been lucky to know kind people, people with good hearts. I saw the darker, hateful side of Lilith, but Daisy got me out of there before the situation became unbearable.

Poor Jake. He didn't have anyone to rescue him from that terrible situation like I did. I turned and looked at his hunched shoulders and hanging head. He'll never have to worry about being whipped again. He's found a good home now.

The next morning when Daisy and Rex came out, instead of placing the halter around my nose, they caught Jake. Before they walked out of the pasture together, Daisy walked over to me and whispered in my ear, "Don't worry, Kobi, I still love you. I just need to work with Brother Jake for a little bit."

Brother Jake? Now, you've got to be kidding me. That enormous beast is not my brother! I bet he doesn't have even a drop of mustang blood in him. How dare you insinuate we're related! Brother? No way!

Of course I didn't get to voice my opinion, not that it would have mattered anyway. 'Brother' Jake, indeed! They must be out of their minds!

*****

Just to show them how unhappy I was to have another horse stealing their attention away from me, I chased after Jake and moved him around every chance I got. Since he was a very lazy horse to start with, chasing him around took more energy on my part than his. That didn't work out nearly as well as I planned, so I started nipping and hitting him with some well-placed kicks to let him know where he stood in the pecking order of my herd. Jake never once complained or tried to become dominant.

Nothing bothered him. He just took whatever I dealt him without emotion. Pretty soon it became pointless, as well as boring, to show Jake I was the lead horse, since he was so obedient about it anyway. He just didn't care. Since it didn't seem that my new big brother would be leaving the herd anytime soon, we settled in and got to know each other.

Once I got over my initial jealousy of Jake, he started telling me his long, depressing tale. In the evenings after Daisy and Rex went home, as we shared a roll of hay, he talked. He said he was only seven years old, but he had seen more pain and suffering in those short years than most horses ever suffered in their entire lifetime.

Jake's life had begun simply enough. He was born in Kentucky on a farm that bred and raised only the Percheron breed of horse. His mother was a beautiful dapple-gray mare, slightly smaller than most of the other Percherons. His father was a huge bay, the largest horse on the farm. The humans bred their largest horse with one of their smallest, hoping the stallion's height would make up for the mare's smaller size.

But, surprise! They ended up with Jake: a bay Percheron with his mother's smaller height and his father's enormous head and feet. Jake obviously had mismatched body parts at birth, and his humans were none too happy about it, either. Jake was allowed to roam free with his mother only until he was weaned. After that he never saw his mother again. At the age of six months, he was shipped off to an auction house.

Jake said he went through a series of humans before he turned three. That's when he was sold to the logging company and his life took a turn for the worse. His training involved a thick heavy collar, worn low on his neck, almost to his withers. The thin straps that held the collar together, buckled at the top of his neck. There was a leather pad that was supposed to rest under the buckle to prevent injury and make the collar less uncomfortable.

To make matters worse, his humans were also lazy and cheap, not wanting to take the time and effort to maintain his equipment or pay to get new collars when the old ones became too worn to be safe or comfortable. Poor Jake was not the only victim of their abuse, but of all the horses in their care, Jake's abuse was the most severe.

The leather pad was missing from his collar. That didn't stop his humans from strapping the collar to his neck and taking him into the mountains to haul out trees. When the buckle started biting into his flesh, Jake would balk, refusing to go forward, because it hurt so much. When he balked, the humans whipped him across his flanks. He was stuck. If he moved forward, the buckle sent blinding pain through his neck. If he stopped, his hide was thrashed with a whip, cutting into his hindquarters and his ribs. Jake could only tolerate the beating for so long before he started pulling again, the metal buckle gouging deeper into his neck.

By the time his workday was over, Jake was a bloody mess from the beatings, as well as from the buckle on the collar digging into his flesh. After work he left a trail of blood all the way down the mountain to his filthy, unkempt stall.

Jake told me he wasn't able to work for a while after that. His humans left him in his filthy stall until all of the signs of their abuse had healed in order to avoid someone seeing it and alerting the authorities to their cruelty. Being left in his disgusting stall for weeks while his body healed was not a good thing either. Day after day of neglect and standing in his own manure and urine took a toll on his feet. The filth became trapped in the hair on his legs and any little scratch on his feet led to infection. By the time the gash on his neck had healed, his feet were so infected and painful that when he stood upright, he could barely stand, much less walk.

It was obvious to his humans at this point Jake would never have a career as a logging horse. The gouge in his neck prevented him from wearing the work collar to haul out trees, and treating his hoof infection was going to cost them more money than they felt he was worth.

They had only one choice: get rid of Jake and let someone else deal with his problems. He was sent to an auction house before the month was out.

Poor Jake. Life continued to be difficult. His mistreatment and abuse had been so brutal and so extreme he feared all things human. He jumped at every sound, any shifts in the light, afraid someone or something was going to hurt him again. The sights and sounds of the auction were enough to send Jake screaming and running away if he could. But, he couldn't. The humans who ran the auctions realized the only way someone would be foolish enough to get involved with a horse his size, and with his fears, was to trick them. So, the morning of the auction, Jake was given a strong sedative to calm him down and take off his nervous edge. Their trick worked! Jake was sold.

A gentle soul called Wyatt bought Jake and moved him further south, into Georgia. He told me that Wyatt was a kind human, almost too kind. He tried to rescue every sorry and pitiful horse he could find and rehabilitate them into functional horses again. Lucky for Jake, Wyatt took a liking to him. Under Wyatt's patience and care Jake healed and developed some trust in humans again. It took some time, but through Wyatt's gentle training, Jake could be ridden and could even jump across small streams or hedges for fox hunting. It cracked me up to imagine big, massive Jake jumping and chasing after a small, sleek fox.

Wyatt was far too compassionate and took in so many horses that some had to go. Since Jake had done so well with his rehabilitation, fox hunting and all, he was one of the first horses to leave.

After Wyatt, Jake went through another series of auctions, meeting more cruel humans who treated him as a piece of property and not a living creature. He lost that little bit of trust he had in humans once again. Eventually he ended up in Florida. That's where he then met the tail-eating donkeys. He stayed with them only a short time, but in that short time they munched his tail into a pitiful, thin line. I've seen thicker twine used to wrap hay, than the bottom of Jake's tail.

The donkeys seemed to think Jake was their equine leader. He told me they followed him everywhere, almost as if he were their king. What a sight—Jake, with his immense size, being surrounded by eight little donkeys. Unfortunately, whenever they got the slightest bit hungry, instead of wandering off to find greener pastures, they would nibble on Jake's tail. I always wondered if they thought about the saying, "you are what you eat," and believed they would grow to Jake's size if they just nibbled enough on his tail.

Jake said his home with the tail-eating donkeys lasted only a few months. His human at the time decided he wanted a horse even larger than Jake, so up for sale Jake went. Lucky for him, Rex was in the market for a horse, and not just any horse would do. Rex is a sizable man. I found that out myself whenever he rode me. Now, I'm not saying Rex was fat. He was tall and carried a good amount of weight because of his height. The first time he rode me, he was worried my skinny little legs would snap like twigs under him. The second time he decided he wanted a more substantial horse to ride. Something really large. Like a draft horse. Like Big Jake!

*****

One warm spring day, the extent of Jake's abusive past and his brutal scars were uncovered for everyone to see. It was one of those hot spring days in Florida that reminded you that the sweltering summer was right around the corner. Daisy decided it was time to body clip poor Jake and cut off his entire long winter coat so he wouldn't have a heat stroke during Florida's sun soaked summer days. When his hair was gone, I saw the scars. Jake's scars ran along the length of his body, all over his ribs and hind-quarters. It was a sad sight to see. Daisy cried when she saw them. I was so thankful that Jake, my gentle giant of a friend, had found his way into a much better family. I was even more thankful I have never felt abuse at the hands of any of the humans I've been involved with. Starvation, yes; abuse, no.

Although his body had healed, Jake's mind still hadn't. One afternoon, after working Jake in the round pen, Daisy had placed us both out to pasture, leaving us alone to eat our evening meal.

"Alright, my little cupcakes, have a wonderful evening and I'll see you bright and early tomorrow morning." Daisy closed the gate behind her.

Jake looked at her and then looked back at me. Between mouthfuls of grain, he mumbled, "Whenever she does that it makes me so nervous."

"Whenever she does what?"

"Calls us food names. You know: Pumpkin, Dumplin', Puddin'. Even when she calls you Coco Bean."

I stopped chewing. "Now, Jake, why in the world would that bother you?"

"Do you think she says stuff like that because she's going to eat us?" Jake was genuinely concerned one night he might become dinner instead of getting to eat it.

I looked over at him, trying to keep a straight face. Eat us? Good grief! "No, Jake, I don't think we have anything to worry about. I think that maybe food is on her mind as much as it's on yours. But, you know, she doesn't always call us food names. Sometimes she calls us Darlin' or Sweetheart, or Sweet Pea. You just never know. Perhaps sometimes she can't remember our names. Don't worry and finish your dinner." I just had to laugh. Food for Daisy!

Over time I came to look at Jake as much more than just another horse or pasture mate. He was my constant companion, my buddy. We were inseparable in the pasture. I found that I would get frantic if I looked around and didn't see his massive body. I would scream until he answered me and let me know he was still within earshot, and nothing tragic had happened to him.

Daisy and Rex started taking the two of us out together onto the wooded trails when we rode and, while Jake depended on me to alert him to any danger I might sense in the woods, I depended

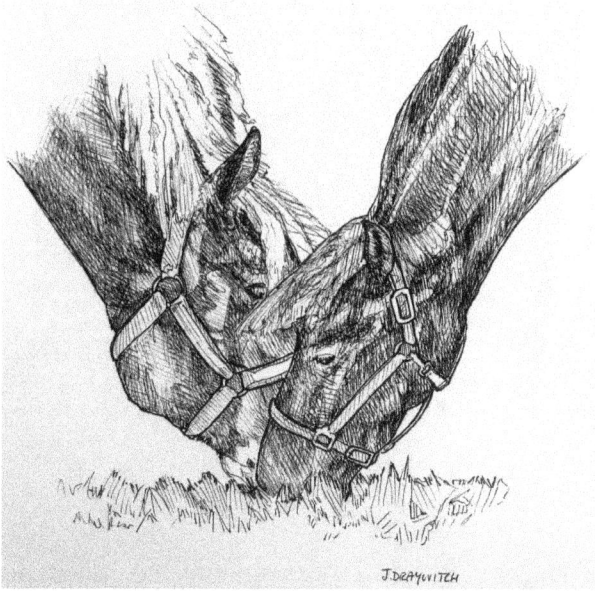

J.DRAYOVITZH

on Jake to always stay behind me and watch my back. He became a faithful friend.

It's hard to admit this, but before I knew that it had happened, I was looking at Jake like I had looked at my herd back in Nevada, as a brother. Yes, a brother! Maybe Rex knew what he was doing after all when he brought Jake home. We were family after all. Daisy, Rex, Kobi, and Jake.

CHAPTER 9 — LET THE SHOW BEGIN

Since Daisy and I had been making so much progress so quickly, our trainer, Wendy, brought up entering me in horse shows.

"I'm serious. I really think you should think about it," Wendy told Daisy one day. "It's not just anyone who can train a wild mustang. What you've done with him is remarkable. I think you should show him."

"I don't know. I showed horses as a kid. My show days are over now. Besides, I just want to ride Kobi for pleasure. I don't have to prove anything to anyone."

"I'm just asking that you consider showing him, that's all."

"Okay, then I've considered it. I'm not gonna do it."

When I heard Daisy say that, I figured my show career was over before it started. It didn't bother me one bit. I'd seen all of those fancy Arabian horses getting ready for their shows by getting their hair cut, having their chin whiskers shaved, and worst of all, having a bath! Ugh! I didn't need any part of that!

Daisy dropped the subject. But, one morning, she was looking for something new and exciting to do when we rode. Bianca, the young girl who popped my rump during the wash rack incident, suggested that since Daisy always rode using a western saddle, for a change we should try Bianca's dressage saddle. Just for fun.

The dressage saddle fit on my back differently than my western one. It also kept Daisy perched farther forward than I was used to. It wasn't bad, just different.

Daisy rode me with that saddle, only two or three times around the arena, and then she headed us back to the barn.

"That was quick," Bianca said. "What's wrong?"

"My back hurts so bad right now I can hardly move. The only thing I can think of is that I'm not used to your dressage saddle. I gotta get down."

"Ooh! Since Kobi's already tacked up, can I ride him?"

"Be my guest." Daisy handed my reins over to Bianca and hobbled back to the barn to sit down.

Excited, Bianca hopped up into the saddle and we headed back out to the arena. She put me through all of my paces: walk, trot and canter. We had a great time together. I was sweating and breathing a little heavy when she brought me back to the barn.

"Thank you for letting me ride him. It was so much fun! He's a lot different and a lot more fun than riding my own stupid horse. Kobi's so smart. And since he's so little I'm not afraid of falling off. He's not scary to ride at all!"

Again, I'm not that little! What's wrong with you guys?

"Well, Bianca, anytime you want a change of pace feel free to work him if I'm not out here. Experiencing someone else's riding style and habits would be great for Kobi."

That day after Bianca left the barn, Wendy walked up to Daisy. "I overheard you telling Bianca she can work Kobi whenever she wants. Thank you. I think Kobi would be a great horse for her to ride to get her confidence back."

"What do you mean, get her confidence back? I didn't know Bianca had lost it. She did really well up on Kobi today."

"On Kobi, yes, I bet she did well. Unfortunately, on her own horse she doesn't. That big thoroughbred of hers gets so stupid sometimes, she can't ride him out of it and ends up falling off. Now if she's riding her horse and he crow hops, jigs, or even swats at a fly with her up there, she dismounts as quickly as she can. She hasn't been able to show him in the last few shows we've taken them to. If he balks when they enter the ring, she panics and starts crying. We end up scratching the class. It's sad

120

to see a 14-year-old girl who loves horses so much be that rattled by her own horse. You've gotten Kobi pretty even tempered now and I think he'd be good for Bianca to ride. It doesn't hurt that Kobi's about four inches shorter than her horse, either."

From then on, Daisy also let me work with Bianca.

*****

A couple of weeks later, Daisy was untacking me after a particularly intense training session with Wendy, and Bianca was tacking up her horse, getting ready to start her own lesson.

"Daisy, I really think you should show Kobi," Wendy said.

"Nope, like I said before, my show days are behind me. I really don't want to put myself through all of that stress again."

"I'll do it," Bianca piped up with a big smile. "I want to show as many different horses as I can for the experience. I've already been working with him. Come on, please? I love Kobi. It'll be so much fun!" Her words rushed out of her like water from a stream.

"Are you sure?" Daisy asked.

"Of course, I'd love to. I'll be the only one out there showing a wild mustang!"

"But what about your parents? Would they mind if you showed Kobi?"

"I don't see why they would. I mean, I'm already coming out to the barn and riding Kobi. I'll ask them before we sign up, if you want."

"It would make me feel better to know they won't mind. If they don't, then I'd love for you to give Kobi a shot at showing."

"Don't worry. Even if my parents have concerns, I always get what I want. My dad has never been able to tell me *no*." Coming from Bianca, that comment didn't make her sound spoiled; she was a girl who knew what she wanted and her parents wanted to keep her happy.

Bianca was starting to get excited at the thought of showing me. "We have to give him a fancy show name. Just 'Kobi' isn't enough. It has to be catchy and special."

"Ooh! I know," Daisy said, caught up in the mood. "How about 'Kobi Juan Kenobi'? Kobi, because, that's his name. Juan, for his Spanish heritage, and Kenobi? Well that's just funny"

Oh, great, Daisy, now what have you just gotten us into? Showing? A catchy show name? Kobi Juan Kenobi. Are you out of your mind? Why couldn't Bianca have just kept quiet?

That was that. Things didn't change. Daisy still kept coming out and riding, and Wendy still trained us on how to work together as a team. When Daisy wasn't out there, Bianca still worked with me too. I thought the plan for taking me to shows had been put on hold until I found out they were just waiting for the Florida summer temperatures to dip. That's when the show season started.

One afternoon, after the weather had turned cooler, Daisy came out for our typical evening session. But this time, after our ride, she had a small black box that fit in the palm of her hand. She flipped a small switch on the side of the box and it started to vibrate.

The noise startled me and I threw my head up to protect it from the vibrating buzz. The sound nagged my mind: I had heard it before. But where?

"Easy, Kobi. It's alright." Daisy stroked my neck. The box continued to buzz in her hand. "These clippers aren't going to hurt you. They're just going to cut your whiskers and make you even more handsome."

I looked at the clippers wide-eyed and suspicious. I seriously doubted the vibrating, buzzing clippers could make me look any different and not hurt me at the same time.

Daisy laid the clippers on my neck, allowing me to feel the vibrations. It didn't hurt at all, it tickled. Something about it felt very familiar.

Now where did I feel this before? Think!

The vibrations on my neck jarred my memory. My mind flew back to Nevada. I finally remembered that sound.

Wasps! It sounded like thousands of wasps all buzzing at the same time. I had heard that buzzing once before, right after I had been captured off the plains. It was those peculiar wasps that didn't sting from my younger days. I didn't know what it was at the time, but it was definitely the same sound. So those weren't strange wasps after all, they were clippers!

I quickly found out being clipped wasn't so bad, it just tickled my lips, unless Daisy got too close and nicked my skin. That stung a little. But whenever it happened she felt so bad about cutting my skin that I didn't have the heart to make a big deal about it.

It's what happened after the clipping that I hated the most. The wash rack. Not to mention the smell! She coated my skin with a gel that made me stink like some sort of fruity flower. She put this goo in my mane and tail to make it soft.

Hey, Daisy, come on now! I'm a mustang, not some sort of domestic house pet. Mustang is a perfectly acceptable smell: dirt, dust, sweat, with a small hint of citronella fly spray.

She didn't listen. If the shower and the wash rack weren't bad enough, the next day they loaded me onto a horse trailer.

Bianca's own horse, Cinnamon, was going along too, so I felt pretty confident I wouldn't be leaving forever. A small part of me was scared that I was being sent off to an auction, like Jake

124

had been, never to return. I was so relieved when I backed off of the trailer and there was Daisy, waiting to grab my lead rope.

Daisy, you're still with me!

While I was being walked to my stall, I started to get that odd feeling in my stomach again. My stomach was starting to cramp up again like that time I had colic. Daisy, Wendy, and Bianca were working hard to get us settled. They threw down stall shavings, filled our water buckets, and gave us our dinner. Since my stomach was starting to hurt, I wasn't hungry, so I didn't eat.

"Uh, oh. Look at Kobi." Daisy pointed out. "He's not even trying to eat. Something's wrong. You don't think he's trying to colic again, do you?"

"I think he might just be stressed out." Bianca shrugged her shoulder. "Take him for a walk. Let him have a look around. Maybe that'll help calm his nerves and settle him down."

Daisy came into my stall and haltered me up. We walked all around the show grounds, checking out the other horses, the arenas, and the grass. I started relaxing and by then I realized just how hungry I was, so Daisy let me graze for a bit. By the time I made it back to my stall I was feeling myself again and was ready for my dinner. Must have just been my nerves!

I didn't know what to expect the next morning, the big day, my first horse show. Our classes were early in the morning, so I had to be fed and groomed before the sun had risen over the horizon. I was a little nervous and anxious after breakfast, but Daisy's familiar movements while she groomed me calmed my nerves. Daisy asked Ruth to come to the show for moral support and to crest-braid my mane, since Daisy had no idea how to braid. Daisy also refused to cut or trim my long, thick mane, making the task all the more difficult. Ruth had to pull extra tight so it wouldn't fall out right in the middle of our class. Ruth yanked my mane so tightly that I couldn't blink! No worries that I would try and take a nap before the class. Heck, I wouldn't be able to close my eyes for a week! By the time I was all tacked up it was already time to warm up.

As Bianca was lunging me, preparing my mind and body for our first class together, two humans, an adult and child walked by. They were discussing me.

"Oh, look at that cute little pony! I wonder what classes he's going to be in."

Pony? Did they call me a pony? Seriously? Just because I don't lumber around here like one of those skittish, harebrained purebreds doesn't make me a pony! I'll show them! Humph, pony!

I did show them, too! I showed everybody what a mustang can do. It was much easier than I had thought it would be. When Bianca was riding, I dropped into my groove, remembering all that I had learned. I flexed at the poll, I stretched, I gave both the collected and extended trot. In short, I was amazing! The judge noticed too. For my first show I earned scores of 55 points for our first class, which was good for a Second Place ribbon, and 61 points in our second class for First Place ribbon! First and Second Place. Not too shabby for my first time out. Daisy and Bianca were proud of me, and I was, too! The only person who didn't seem proud was Bianca's father. He kept giving me odd looks, like I had two heads growing out of my neck.

When we got home to our barn that afternoon, a couple of humans who were there visiting with their horses came up and asked Daisy how the show went. While Bianca and Daisy bragged about my classes, a teenage boy rode up on his horse with a sneer on his face.

"I don't see what the big deal is about a wild mustang doing dressage. Any old horse can do that stuff. They're born knowing it!"

"Oh, you think so, do you?" Bianca scoffed. "Then you come out here anytime on your horse and I'll be more than happy to you give both you and your horse a lesson. Then we'll see what your domestic horse was born knowing."

We all turned our backs on him and left him standing there with his jaw hanging open, catching flies. I think that boy was just trying to impress Bianca with his opinion on horses. Too bad it had just the opposite effect on her!

*****

The rest of the show season went well. Bianca and I kept earning First and Second Place ribbons. At the end of the Fall Show Season, I overheard Bianca telling Daisy, "Guess what? You're never going to believe it!"

"What? Tell me. What happened?"

"Well," Bianca continued, so excited that she was almost breathless, "Kobi and I earned High Point Champion for our level for the Fall Series!"

"You're kidding! That's great. But what does it mean?"

"It means in only three shows, Kobi scored enough points that we got the highest point total out of all the horses competing in our level. It means that he beat out all of those other horses for the entire series. Can you believe it? High Point Champion!"

"No! Honestly, I never would have thought that a wild mustang would have done so well in dressage."

Well, I knew that I could do it, Daisy. You just had to have a little faith in me and give me a chance!

Since I performed so well in the last three shows, Wendy convinced Daisy to allow Bianca and me to try to qualify for

Championships during the Spring Show Season. We needed three scores above 63. I qualified in my first three rides. Like I said, I was on fire! That meant the fall shows would just be good practice for me before I rode in the final Championship Show in November.

*****

Things continued on an upswing until our second show of the Fall Season. When Bianca and I came out of the ring, Daisy was there to greet me and lead me back to my stall. After taking off my saddle and bridle, Daisy quickly realized I was dripping in sweat and needed to be rinsed off before the next class.

"Ruth, would you help me get Kobi rinsed off? I don't think I can handle Kobi being in a strange place and the wash rack on my own."

She muffled some sort of response.

"Ruth, what's wrong? Are you crying? What's going on?"

"I'm so mad right now. While Kobi was in the ring I overheard Bianca's father saying some really mean and nasty stuff about Kobi during his last class. He didn't even care that I was standing there hearing him. In fact, he was talking loud enough for everyone over there to hear him."

"What did he say?" Daisy asked. I could tell just by the way Daisy asked the question that she was about to go on the warpath. I could even picture her face without needing to see it: her eyes would go squinty, she'd scrunch up her eyebrows where they would almost meet in the middle, and her lips would pucker. I'd seen that look before and it wasn't pretty!

Ruth dropped her voice, making it sound deeper than it was normally, and pretended to be Richard. It was so funny. I snickered to myself, until I heard the words he used.

"My daughter, Bianca, is so much better than that little horse. I don't know why she still rides him. He messes with her head and she's not going anywhere with him. She should just focus on her own horse. What's the point of riding him in the championships, anyway? He's not going to win."

Ruth switched back into her normal voice, "I walked up to him and told that him it mattered to you."

Ruth puffed herself back up, dropped her voice and pretended to be Richard again. "Hmmh! Bianca's riding skills are way beyond that mustang. She should be riding much better horses than him. He's just not up to her standards."

At that point, Ruth knew she'd never change Richard's closed mind and couldn't handle any more of his hateful talk. She stormed away from him and looked for Daisy.

What Richard said made my blood boil. I think Daisy's blood was boiling right up there with mine, but she expressed her anger differently. After Wendy came back in from calling Bianca's other class, she found Ruth and Daisy next to my stall, deep in whispered conversation.

"What's goin' on, Daisy? You're mad about something."

"I've decided I'm pulling Kobi from the next class and the Championships."

"What?" Wendy seemed confused.

Daisy, you decided what? I don't want to get pulled. I earned it. I want to do those classes. Isn't that what we're here for? Isn't that why we've worked so hard? Don't let them talk you out of it! I can prove them all wrong. Trust me.

"Ruth just overheard Richard saying some hateful things about Kobi."

"And?" Wendy asked.

"Richard doesn't think Kobi is quality enough for Bianca to ride him. He thinks that she's better than Kobi and he's a step down for her. Richard forgets that it was Kobi who got Bianca's confidence back in the first place." Daisy was so angry. Her face was still scrunched up and she was spitting out her words.

Wendy sighed, choosing her words carefully. "So what? We don't really care what he thinks, now do we? Honestly, what does he know? He's the idiot who bought her that big crazy thoroughbred that rattled her so much in the first place. If it weren't for the horse that *he* bought her, her confidence would be just fine."

Yeah...what does Richard know anyway? He obviously doesn't know a good horse when he sees one.

"We all know what Richard said isn't true," Wendy continued. "You and Kobi have worked hard, including helping Bianca get over that fear she had of showing with her horse. You and I both know that."

And I know it too!

"So," Wendy went on, "what's the best way to prove him wrong?"

"That's just it. We don't need to prove anything to Richard or anyone anymore. If Kobi's not quality enough to be here, I just want to take him home." There was a hitch in Daisy's voice, like she was about to cry.

"You're missing the point. You and I know both know what Kobi is capable of doing. He's already proved it. If you pull him out now, Richard wins. You have to keep Kobi in this show. I know the first class didn't go as well as you had hoped. With all of this rain we've been having, it's been difficult for him to be worked. Just leave him in today as practice for the Championships next month. Kick butt in the Championships and prove to Richard and to everyone else—and I do mean everyone else—once and for all that a mustang has the quality to be here competing, and winning, against all of these purebred horses."

Go, Wendy!

"Okay." Daisy conceded, not quite convinced yet, but smart enough to let Wendy's words soak in. "I know that Kobi is amazing. I'll let the rest of them find out at the next show."

As if she'd been standing around the corner listening, Bianca came storming up the barn isle. "I just heard," she fumed. "Daisy, don't listen to a word my father said! I love him, but sometimes he's an idiot. Don't you dare pull Kobi from the shows. I want to ride him all the way into the Championships. He's already qualified for it, and we're doing it." She didn't even wait for an answer; she just turned on her heel and marched back out.

"Well," Wendy laughed, "I guess that's settled. Now, quit stomping around here like a wounded bear. Take a deep breath, cool down, and get Kobi ready for his next class."

Finally it was time for our last class of the day. We didn't do as well as I had hoped. There was too much drama and emotion surrounding the ride. Everyone was too flustered from the morning's events to give it our best performance. I blame Richard for that, but we still managed to pull out a 49. Daisy thought the judge's comments about the ride were hilarious: "Difficult ride due to tension!"

Tension? That judge didn't know the half of it!

After the last class, Bianca came up to Daisy as she was brushing me down and wrapping my legs for the ride home.

"We have a slight problem."

Oh, no. Now what? I don't think I can deal with any more human problems today!

I could feel Daisy's body tense. She stopped wrapping my legs and took a deep breath. Not bothering to stand up, Daisy rested her head against my shoulder and sighed. "What's the problem now?"

"For whatever reason, my dad really doesn't like Kobi."

"Hmmph, you don't say." Daisy replied, quiet enough where I was the only one to hear her.

"Dad said he won't drive me to the barn on weekends anymore if I'm going to ride Kobi. That means I'll only be able to ride one day during the week and won't have time to ride more than my horse. I don't know what to do. I really want to take Kobi to the Championships; we earned that. I have to be the one to ride him; we can't transfer his points to another rider now." Bianca's voice just trailed off.

Still resting her head on my shoulder, Daisy gave another huge sigh. I knew her well enough by now to know that her mind was racing trying to think of a solution to this latest problem.

Standing up, Daisy looked over my neck to Bianca, "How about if I come out and pick you up early on Sunday mornings.

We'll grab a bite to eat on our way out to the barn. You can work Kobi first. I'll untack, groom him, and finish him up while you work your horse. Then I'll wait for you to finish up and take you back home. This way you'll get to work Kobi one day a week, your horse two days a week, and your father won't have to be involved."

"You know, I think that'll work great. Let's give it a shot! Championships are only a month away. We can make anything work for a month."

*****

For the next four weeks, Daisy was out every day to work me and to make sure I was in perfect shape for Championship Show. Bianca rode me on Sundays and Daisy took care of me when the ride was over. I enjoyed all the attention and worked hard for both of them. I knew my reputation and that of mustangs everywhere was at stake.

With all of our hard work, there was nothing that could stop me from proving that I was worthy, high quality, and had earned the right to be at Championships. Bring it on!

CHAPTER 10 — CHAMPIONSHIP

It was the morning of the Championship show. When Daisy got to the show grounds it was still dark and so cold my breath came out in white puffs. I nickered to her so she could find me in the dark stable.

"Oh, there you are, Kobi," she whispered. "Ready for breakfast, my little champion?"

Ready? Are you kidding? I'm always *ready for breakfast*!

I heard her scoop the grain out of the bag and pour it into my bucket. I nickered to her again so she would know just how hungry I was.

While I was happily munching away on the sweet grain, Daisy started to curry all of the stall shavings from my body. I could sense her nerves were on edge, so I understood why sometimes she rubbed me just a bit too hard. She would lighten

136

up whenever I stopped eating and turned my head to glare at her. Thankfully, Wendy and Ruth showed up to take over the finishing touches before Daisy could rub all the hair off my body. Bianca stood back to keep herself clean for the show.

After I was groomed, braided and all tacked up, Bianca and I headed out to warm up. As we were walking out of the barn, she stopped to pick up the lunge line and whip.

Ugh! I hate running around in a circle. What's the point? It's the dumbest thing we have to do. I'd rather not.

I was getting angry and frustrated at just the thought of lunging. I tossed my head around and pawed at the ground.

"Hey, Bianca?" Daisy followed us out into the dawning morning. "I have an idea. Since lunging makes Kobi so mad, why don't we skip it for now? If he doesn't settle in, lunge him, but first give him a shot at warming up under saddle."

Oh, yeah! That's a great idea—skip lunging.

I held my breath to see what Bianca would decide to do.

"I guess we can give it a try. Keep this with you, just in case." She handed Daisy the hated lunge line and whip.

Nah, you won't need that. No lunging. I'll make sure of it.

I did everything Bianca asked me to do. And I did it the first time she asked. I didn't want to take any chances she would feel the need to lunge me. I kept my head tucked perfectly as we went through our pattern. I walked when Bianca wanted, trotted when

137

she asked, and stopped when she requested. We performed beautifully. I knew this was my day to really shine. It was my last show: The Championships. Daisy, Wendy, and Bianca had worked me hard to prepare for this day. They believed in me. I was not going to let them down. They were counting on me to prove Richard wrong – again.

"Come on, Kobi," Bianca said. "It's showtime. It's our turn to go in."

Showtime! I felt my pulse quicken. *This was it!*

I trotted into the ring. My head was tucked down, my tail raised, my feet moving out. I felt on top of the world. We halted for the salute. I bowed to the judge as well; it couldn't hurt! I trotted out again. I didn't cut the circles short or sway from the center line. I stretched as low as I could, trying to graze the sand with my nose. I gave it all I had. Bianca was quick to correct me any time my nose came out or my head came up and I responded to her hands each time. We worked together well and I knew it was beautiful. Then before I knew it, we were halting again for our final salute. Whew! It was over fast. I had done the best I could. The only thing left was to wait for the scores.

Daisy met us as we left the arena. "You were beautiful, Kobi," she whispered, "just beautiful."

I looked over at her to see why she was whispering. There were tears in her eyes. "I'm so proud of you." She looked up at Bianca and added, "Thank you."

Then Holly and Wendy came up, and they were crying too! Everyone wept and started hugging each other, all the while saying that they couldn't believe it.

I could believe it! I knew all along I had it in me. I just didn't see why I had to prove it to all those other humans I didn't know. A little faith, please!

Bianca dismounted. Daisy took my reins and led me back to my stall. We only had one ride, so I was able to rest now. I was untacked, groomed, watered, and given a snack. Life was good!

It seemed as if we had to wait forever to find out the results. They made us wait until the official awards ceremony in the afternoon to tell us our score.

Then, finally it was time to get groomed and tacked up again. As soon as we were ready, we headed back to the arena. Since I wasn't performing again, there was no need to warm up. I just had to stand and wait until it was our turn to go in for the scores. After what seemed like an eternity, they waved us to enter.

Bianca and I walked into the center of the ring, turned, and faced the judges. While we waited for the other horses to enter, the judges were scurrying about, as if they were still trying to figure out what they were doing.

*Come on, the suspense is killing me. Just tell us how **we** did.*

I didn't let my impatience show, though. I was as calm as I could be, standing in one spot, not moving or dancing like I normally do. I tried with all my might to will them to hurry up.

"Ladies and Gentlemen," a voice announced from the sky. "First place, Champion, with 64 points, goes to Katie Nichols on Little Dreamer. Great job, Katie."

What? 'Katie' sounds like 'Kobi'. Was it us? Did he say my name wrong?

Lost in my thoughts, I almost missed the next announcement.

"Second place, Reserve Champion, with a score of 63 points, goes to Bianca Holt on Kobi Juan Kenobi."

I didn't hear anything after that. I barely noticed Bianca stroking my neck and didn't hear how any of the other horses in our class did.

63 points! Second place! Reserve Champion! I knew I done my best, and the judges noticed!

Before long, it was time for us to get our enormous ribbons. Being Reserve Champion meant I got to wear the big red and gold ribbon around my neck. Little Dreamer was the Champion, so he was awarded his blue ribbon first. But he wasn't having any part of it. Each time they tried to put the ribbon around his neck, he would back away.

What was wrong with him? Didn't he know that he was the Champion and that it was an honor to get to wear the ribbon? It was something to be proud of, not afraid of. Silly horse! They finally gave up and handed Little Dreamer's ribbon over to his rider, who draped it across her shoulders like a sash.

Now it was my turn to get a ribbon and I didn't move a muscle. I stood proudly and completely still so they could get the ribbon around my neck without misplacing my mane. I did drop my head down a little to make it easier for them to fasten it.

I could almost hear my old herd from Nevada laughing at me. They were wild and free, and here I was with my mane braided, smelling like strawberries, and wearing a huge ribbon around my neck, all with a human on my back. While it certainly wasn't the life they would have chosen, I was glad it was mine. I showed everyone that my mustang brothers were capable of achieving anything if they had the proper attitude and the right human willing to work with them and give them a chance.

As soon as the ribbon was in place the judge moved out of the way so people could take our picture. I know I looked handsome. My coat gleamed in the sunlight, my perfectly braided mane and forelock showed the lines on my face and neck, and that big red and gold ribbon glistened around my neck. There wasn't a mustang between here and Nevada who looked any better than I did at that moment. I was sure of it!

After the others had received their ribbon, it was time for our victory lap around the ring. We were supposed to go in order of ribbon: the Champion went first, followed by me, the Reserve Champion, and then the others.

We started out that way, but Little Dreamer was going too slow. To keep things moving, I was going to have to pass him. The way I looked at it, since Little Dreamer wouldn't wear his ribbon, I should be first in line anyway. So I passed him. Bianca, though, had other ideas. Before I knew it, she had me trotting around in a circle so Little Dreamer could keep his lead. We were back in second place.

What an injustice! I was just trying to take my rightful place.

142

We followed Little Dreamer out of the arena, and we stopped at Daisy's side. She was crying again. Within seconds, here came Holly and Wendy, and they were crying again too.

I swear, I have never seen humans cry so much in one day.

I may have finished in second place, but I knew in Daisy's heart I was her Champion.

As she led me back to my stall, with my enormous 'Reserve Champion' ribbon slung across my shoulder, we walked directly past that jerk, Richard. I saw Daisy square her shoulders as she made herself walk taller. As we passed him we both had the same thoughts. Under her breath, I heard Daisy's "Humph!" She didn't look over at Richard or make any kind of eye contact. She just kept walking, proudly, with her head held high. I didn't look in his direction either. I walked past him, holding my head high, too, and my tail a little higher. Daisy and I were quite a pair.

Not quality? Well, Richard, what do you think of me now?

When we got back to my stall, Daisy threw herself around my neck.

"Kobi," she whispered, "you did it! You proved that a wild mustang has every right to be in dressage. You proved Richard and any other mustang-hating idiots wrong!"

Daisy fed me a handful of treats to show me how happy she was. Next came all of the photos with Bianca: me wearing the ribbon while tacked up, me wearing the ribbon untacked, me wearing the ribbon in the show ring, me wearing the ribbon while standing under a huge American flag…you get the idea. I loved every minute of it, too. I was Kobi, the Reserve Champion!

Finally it was time to go home. Daisy and Wendy were determined to get me into the tall red trailer, but I was just as determined I wasn't going to get in. It wasn't my normal trailer. Plus, there wasn't another horse in it. What was going on? Why should I go? I liked all this fuss over me and wanted to stay here.

Finally I relented and I ended up getting into the red trailer all by myself. It was a lonely ride home.

We pulled all the way into the breezeway when we got back to the barn, but no one was hurrying to let me out of the trailer. In fact, for some reason Daisy had grabbed Jake's halter and jogged out to the pasture to get him. Shortly she returned, leading Jake towards the trailer. The other side of the trailer opened and Daisy tried to lead Jake into the trailer with me. I was so confused.

I'm ready to get off, now. Why are you loading Jake? What's going on?

It took Jake a few tries and some sweet feed, but before long he was my partner in the red trailer. I felt the ground start to move and we were off again. This was strange. Where were we going? What was happening? At least I wasn't alone this time. Whatever was going on, Jake and I were in it together.

After a short and bumpy ride, we stopped. I had no idea where we were. Daisy hopped out and tried to get Jake's head loose so he would be the first one out. Fine by me! Jake can check this new place out first. If he doesn't like it, then I just won't get out of the trailer.

"Jake's ready!" I heard Daisy shout, "Come and catch his head as he backs out."

"I got him." Rex hollered back. "Let him out!"

Rex? Rex is here at this new place too? What's going on? Where are we?

Daisy came around and clipped the lead rope to my halter. "Ok, Kobi's ready." The door behind my rump opened and I slowly backed out of the trailer. Jake wasn't in any distress and Rex was here, so this place couldn't be too bad. Could it?

At last I was out and back on solid ground. I looked around and saw Jake was already grazing, with Rex holding on the other end of his lead rope. Daisy held my rope, but I wasn't interested in grazing, I needed to look around and figure out where I was. Wendy was there, too, and was busy giving Daisy directions as I led her around the pasture to check out the new surroundings. Then Wendy got out some bags of feed, and that really got my attention.

There's feed! Were we going to be staying here?

I was still checking out my new surroundings, when I saw something out of the corner of my eye, moving towards us. Fast. I spun around to face the fast moving threat. Blowing hard to get its scent.

"It's okay Kobi, it's just Cuzzin. You remember him."

Oh, right. The dumb dog you like to keep around for some reason. I thought you would have gotten rid of him by now.

I was pulled out of my thoughts when I heard Daisy tell Rex and Wendy, "Okay, let's go to the barn, put them in their stalls and get them settled."

A barn? Stalls? We have stalls here? Yes! We are going to be staying here!

Daisy and Rex led Jake and me around back to a little two-stall barn. Aha! The mystery was unfolding. It was just going to be the two of us living here. When Jake and I got in, we found the two largest stalls I had ever seen. They were twice as large as any other stall I'd been in, and completely covered with wood shavings. Wow! This new place was pretty nice. And then Daisy and Rex fed us dinner.

Barn! Stalls! Wood shavings! Food! I love it here!

*****

It had only been a few wonderful and relaxing months since that wonderful evening before I realized that every morning, when I woke up, I would have Daisy there to feed me. Imagine!

Life had slowed down now. No more cold, stinky, perfume-filled baths, short haircuts, or long, hot sweaty workouts. The only thing I have to put up with now is that dumb dog Cuzzin. I pay him back though. Each time he tries to sneak out and run away, I'm always watching. This way whenever Daisy looks for him, all she has to do is watch where I'm looking. She's caught that stupid dog every single time!

I'm fortunate enough to spend most of my days with my big brother Jake, eating the lush grass in the green pastures. I spend all of my nights comfortably in my stall crunching hay into the wee hours of the morning. It doesn't get much better than this.

I would have been content to live this way forever, but I should have known by now that things never stay perfect. Life always has a way of changing and surprising you.

CHAPTER 11 — FOUNDER

Life was perfect until that one cool, rainy day. The day started brilliantly. The sun was shining and there was a nip in the air, signaling the brutal Florida summer was finally coming to an end. To top it off, there wasn't a bug around for miles to bite me. In short, it was a great day to be a horse!

Around mid-day, storm clouds started rolling in and Daisy took that as her cue to put Big Jake and me in our stalls. I love it when we get to go in our stalls before the rain comes, instead of after we are already wet. I think she's finally realized how much I hate getting wet. I've overhead her tell Rex the main reason Jake and I go to our rooms when it rains, is because Jake has something wrong with his hooves and they have to stay dry. While I know Jake's hooves are Daisy's main concern, I know in the back of her mind she also knows how much I hate being wet. I know she's also doing it for me because she wants me to be as comfortable and happy as I can be. I really love Daisy!

Anyway, even after we were put up, it was still a good day. Daisy gave us a mid-afternoon bran mash for a snack and kept coming out to give us enough hay to keep us busy. That afternoon, when the rain was starting to slow down, Jake started grumbling that his belly was beginning to hurt.

"Kobi, I don't feel so good. My belly feels all tight and my hooves are hurting. I think I'm going to lay down for a little bit."

Uh-oh. I've had a stomachache only once in my life before; it was one of the worst experiences of my life. I didn't want to tell Jake that and scare him, since he had enough to think about with his stomach, but I decided to keep my eye on him until Daisy came back out to check on us. She helped me to feel better last time; I knew she'd be able to help Jake. I just wished she'd hurry up.

A little while later, the rain had stopped, the sun was trying to peek back out. Daisy came to let us out of our stalls. Jake was doing more than lying down, he was laid out. His entire body was on the ground, his neck was stretched out, and his head rested in the stall shavings. Daisy went into action, like I knew she would.

"Jakey, honey, what's wrong?"

Jake raised his head in response to her voice, but didn't answer her.

He's sick. His stomach hurts. Come on, Daisy. You know what to do.

Daisy wasn't listening to me. She got out our cookies like she always does when she wants to make sure we still want to eat. Jake didn't show the least bit of interest in the cookies, showing just how sick he was. If the big guy didn't want to eat cookies, it was bad.

My own stomach rumbled when the sweet smell of the cookies reached my nose.

Hey! Don't forget me over here. I still want my cookies!

Daisy heard my nicker that time and gave me a handful of the sweet snacks. She led me out of my stall to the front field to turn me loose to graze. I knew when she left that she was going back to the barn to get Jake up. I knew he was in good hands, so I tried not to worry anymore. After being in my stall all morning, I was hungry. I waited a few minutes for Jake to join me. When he didn't come I knew he was still with Daisy, so I found a good place to graze and started eating.

A little later, Daisy walked around with Jake. He was wearing his halter and Daisy was leading him with his lead rope. He started sniffing the ground like he was going to start grazing, but lay back down instead.

This isn't good. Come on, Jake. Time to get up and start eating again.

He answered me by trying to roll.

Come on, Daisy, do something!

She heaved, tugged, and pulled Jake back up into a standing position, and started walking him around. I saw her get a box the size of her hand out of her pocket and start talking into it.

"Hey, Wendy, it's Daisy. I've got a problem here with Jake. I think he's trying to colic."

Oh, no. Not colic. I remember that's the bad stomachache I had. Give him that shot. It will make him feel better. It worked for me, remember?

Before my thoughts were complete, Daisy was yelling into the house. "Rex! Grab me the shot of banamine out of the fridge, and bring it out here please."

Daisy let Jake lay down again, as long as he promised not to roll anymore. I think he would have promised anything so long as he could lie down. While he was lying there, she went ahead and gave him the shot. "That's it, Jakey. In about 20 minutes, you'll be as good as new again. Just relax."

Sure enough, in a little while, Jake got to his feet again. I was glad. Before long, my stomach was telling me it was dinner time. Daisy brought us back to our stalls for a light dinner.

"How are you feeling Jake?" I asked him after we ate.

"Better. But something just doesn't feel right. I can't figure out exactly what it is, Kobi, but I just feel tired and icky."

I was somewhat relieved knowing Jake was eating, and seemed to be improving even if he was tired and icky. It didn't last long though. He felt poorly for the next few days. It didn't matter what Daisy tried. It would work for a little while and then he would stop eating and lay down again.

I continued my watch over him. Every time he would lie down, I would go and stand next to him so I could protect him and make sure nothing would attack him. Once again, he laid himself out, with his head resting flat on the ground. I didn't like that. Not one bit. I had only seen one other horse do that, and that was when I was still running wild in Nevada.

Back then, one of the older mares had gotten sick and lay down like that. When the herd was ready to move on, she didn't get up. With the safety of the herd at stake, we couldn't wait for her to get back to her feet. Mother told me we had to leave the old mare behind. "It is the way of life," Mother said. "Survival of the strongest. She is old and not strong anymore. We have to leave her here." When we left, I turned to take one last look at the old mare I had known since I was born. She was up on her feet again, yet slowly walking the opposite way that the herd was going.

I told Mother the mare was back on her feet. Mother stopped and turned, watching the old mare stumbling away from us. "She's going to find someplace peaceful to lie down forever, son. Come, we must go and rejoin our herd."

Thinking back to that day with Mother and the old mare, I got scared. I couldn't leave Jake behind; he was the only other horse in my herd. He had to get to his feet.

Once Jake lay down for entirely too long, I got nervous and started screaming at him to make him get back up. I ran over to him to nip him, kick him, whatever it was going to take to get him up. Before I could reach him, Jake got to his feet. Feeling pretty smug that I got him up, I turned my back on him for a few moments. When I looked back to check on him, he was gone. I panicked!

"Jake! Jake, where are you?" I started running all around the pasture looking for him. I screamed his name the whole time. He wasn't up front. He wasn't on the side eating hay. He wasn't back at the barn. Where was he? He had just disappeared.

I was running laps around the entire property. I had to find Jake. What if he lay down again and I couldn't find him to help get him up? As I was rounding the corner by the barn, I spied Daisy leading Jake out of the wooded part of the pasture. Jake never goes in the trees. Why did he go in there? I realized it didn't matter why he wandered in there. Daisy found him and he was standing up. Jake was okay. Whew! What a scare.

Before the sun set that night, Daisy and Rex went to spend some extra time with Jake. I tried not to be jealous. I knew Jake wasn't feeling good, but I was starting to be annoyed with all of the attention he was getting. Daisy hardly spent any time with me since he got sick. It seemed all she thought about was Jake, Jake, and Jake. While he is my friend and brother, Daisy is my human. I needed some time with her too.

Before I could get too angry with Jake, he yelled to me, "Kobi? Are you there?"

"Yeah, I'm over here."

"I don't feel so good."

That pushed all of my mean thoughts about Jake away and I ran over to him, past a very surprised Daisy, who had wandered away from him and was finally coming to see me. Right now, they were right: Jake is the top priority.

*****

Jake stayed like that, not feeling good but not in severe pain either. Until the next day. Then he got worse. The day started well for him, he was even trying to nibble on some grass, when all of a sudden his hooves really started hurting. Now, Jake has always had bad hooves, so hearing him stomp and fuss about them was nothing new. By dinner time, though, Jake couldn't walk straight. He couldn't move his back legs in motion with his front legs. It was almost as if someone had stuck two different horses together and they didn't know what each end was doing.

Daisy and Rex had to lead him back into the barn. It was painful to watch and I can only imagine how painful it was for poor Jake. He was shuffling like an old horse...a very old horse. He dragged his hooves when he could and hopped on his others when he had to. Hop, drag, hop. They finally made it to Jake's stall where he could eat his dinner.

"Kobi, it's bad. My hooves have never hurt like this before. I don't know what to do."

"Neither do I. Maybe you just have something stuck in them. Once Daisy picks your hooves they'll feel better."

"There's nothing in my hooves. She looked when we were out in the pasture. They hurt so bad that I didn't want her picking them up. I'm telling you Kobi. There is something seriously wrong with me."

"I'm sure you're fine." I told him, trying to make him feel better. "We'll go for a walk to the front pasture after dinner, and see how you feel then."

Daisy didn't give Jake a chance to walk into the front pasture. She kept him in the back yard, closer to her, closer to the barn, but farther from me. I tried not to panic. I could still see him and smell him. He'd be fine. He had to be.

When Wendy showed up, I knew I was wrong; Jake wasn't fine. When Holly, Daisy's mother showed up, I knew things must be really bad for poor Jake. I had no idea what they were doing when they put Jake's front hooves in buckets of ice, but I had to trust them that they knew what they were doing. Jake either trusted them or was too sick to care what they did. He didn't put up a fuss, and allowed them to keep his front hooves in the ice.

For the first time in a long time, I was put in my stall without having Jake across the barn aisle in his when the sun went down. I was confused and scared for my friend and brother.

Once the sun had set and the moon was high in the sky, things really got lively. Another human showed up, one I had never met. She had the smell of sickness and medicine on her. She stepped up and seemed to take charge. She told everyone they had done the right thing by putting Jake's hooves in ice; hopefully it relieved some of the swelling of laminitis and might have prevented him from foundering.

I had never heard of 'laminitis' or 'foundering' before, but it wasn't long until everyone who was at the barn that night knew what it was. Bad!

The next day, before I had been given a chance to be turned out to graze for the day, there were even more humans out there.

Wendy and Holly had left, but Daisy, Rex and some different humans that smelled like sickness and medicine were out. They made Jake stand on pieces of wood so they could take pictures of his hooves. It hurt Jake to move, but he tried his best to put his hooves where they wanted him to. They also stuck something into Jake's neck and stitched it into place. The smelly human explained to Daisy that Jake would need to keep the big needle in his neck for three days so he could get medicine to help his hooves. Daisy would need to give him medicine through the needle in his neck four times a day during that time.

Poor Daisy. She had a smell of sickness about her too. Whenever she would talk, her voice sounded as if she had been eating hay all day without drinking any water. She had a tiredness in her eyes that I had never seen before. Still, I knew that Daisy, being Daisy, would take care of Jake first, before taking care of herself.

The results of the pictures of Jake's hooves were done while the sun was still high in the sky. I overheard Daisy talking into that strange box she kept in her pocket. She was crying.

"Jake's foundered. The best I can understand from what the vets have told me and what I've read is that last night when he couldn't walk, he had a bad case of laminitis. What's laminitis? Oh, sorry. There's something called 'lamina' in his hoof. It separates the hoof from the hoof wall. For whatever reason, it swelled. When the swelling went down, the bone in the hoof, called the coffin bone, can rotate and drop. If the coffin bone drops, that's founder. That's what happened to poor Jake. The bone can continue to drop for up to a week. In a worst case scenario, the bone can actually penetrate through the bottom of his hoof. If that happens, there's nothing we can do for him." Daisy started crying so hard she couldn't talk anymore. She put the box back in her pocket and went into Jake's stall, where he was lying down, to give him a hug.

"Oh, Jakey, what are we going to do?" Daisy sobbed into his thick mane.

Wait a minute. What do you mean there's nothing you can do for him? Come on Daisy, think! A bone coming through his hoof? That's going to hurt him. Think of something!

*****

But things seemed to be getting worse for Jake. I started hanging out around the barn to comfort him and to overhear Daisy, either when people came to visit or when she was talking into that box. By hanging out and listening, I learned more than I ever wanted to. The first thing I found out was that the humans who smelled like sickness and medicine were called 'vets.'

When another vet came out the next day, he told Daisy that things weren't looking good for Jake. A horse his size would never fully recover from founder.

"I personally would never own a draft horse that had foundered," the vet said. "They have just too much weight on their feet. I'd have him put down."

What is that? Put down? Jake lays down all the time, so he's fine, right?

Daisy started crying.

"Before you do something like that, give him one week. He's on enough pain medication right now so that he's not suffering too much. Allow him time to rally and let nature take its course. See what he can do. We'll come out tomorrow to give him the final IV, and the rest will be up to him."

Daisy nodded in agreement, unable to speak through her tears and her still raspy voice.

"But you have to take care of yourself too. I can tell you're pretty sick also. Go inside and rest. You've done all you can for Jake right now. He needs to rest and so do you."

Daisy nodded again, thanked the vet for coming out and, against the vet's orders, went back to the barn to spend time with Jake.

By the next week, both Daisy and Jake were recovering. Daisy had lost the smell of sickness around her, and Jake was able to leave his stall for almost an hour a day to come out and graze. All in all, things were looking up.

As winter turned colder, Jake became stronger. He was able to stay out of his stall almost all day, laying down to rest when he needed to, and before long, he was grazing out in the front pasture with me again. Even so, he was different. He was much slower and acted much older than he had been before he'd gotten sick. He was slow and stiff, like a very old horse. Poor Jake.

CHAPTER 12 — SHOWING AGAIN

Once spring came and the new, tender grasses started shooting up all over the pasture, Wendy came out and paid Daisy a visit. The women were sitting on the front porch, enjoying the warm day, when I heard Wendy say the words I never thought I'd hear again: "horse show."

That got my attention. *Seriously, Daisy? Showing again? Are you out of your mind? You said we were retired!*

"I think Kobi would make a great little western pleasure horse." Wendy told Daisy.

Oh, and not even show dressage? Watch it with those "little horse" comments there, too.

"Riding out here by yourself has made both you and Kobi a little soft."

What's wrong with being soft? Daisy, you're not saying anything. Are you actually considering this?

"The next show isn't until March, so you have plenty of time to get prepared. It will give both of you a goal to work towards. It'll be good for you guys and will help get your mind off Jake, not to mention how much fun you'll have."

"Hmph! Fun isn't the first word that pops into my mind when I think of shows. Hard work, long days, stress, but not usually fun. Besides, this time it's all on me. Bianca's not around to ride him anymore."

You know, now that you mention it, I haven't seen Bianca since we moved here. Where is she?

"Her dad wouldn't have let her ride Kobi anyway. Now that his sights are set on getting her into the Olympics, it's warmbloods or nothing." Wendy said.

Oh, yeah. Her dad – it's all becoming clear now.

*****

After the first lesson with Wendy, I decided I liked western pleasure much better than dressage. It's slower for one thing. I could jog all day long and not wear myself out. I was surprised such a great idea had come from Wendy, but of course I'll never let on I was enjoying myself. Daisy and I still spent a lot of time

162

in the woods trail riding, so I never really had a chance to get bored with all the schooling again.

One afternoon, after a lesson where I had performed spectacularly, Daisy and Wendy were discussing the upcoming show.

"What classes do you think we should enter? They have classes for novice riders as well as green horses."

I'm going to suggest we enter novice rider, since I'm not a green horse; I'm black. I shook my head, laughing a little. *I swear Daisy; you see me every day and still don't know what color I am?*

"You're not a bad rider. Even though you haven't shown in years and have never shown Kobi, I think you should go with green horse. He's still young and doesn't have any experience with western shows, so the judges will probably be more forgiving if he makes a mistake."

Me? Make a mistake? I usually don't make mistakes; I may make bad decisions, but those are intentional! Mistakes? Never!

"Green horse it is then," Daisy answered as she and Wendy made their way out of the barn to finalize the plans for the show.

*****

Even though Daisy was keeping things low key, I could tell we were gearing up for a show. Wendy came out several times a week and worked us to a sweat. I enjoyed the times without Wendy much more. Daisy and I would head into the woods, just the two of us. I knew what Daisy was up to. We still practiced our jog and weaved in between trees, yet I think she just enjoyed the change of scenery. I did too.

I started to get nervous when Daisy gave me a bath. I knew show time was coming close. When Wendy came with a horse trailer loaded up with a mare to stay and keep Jake company, I knew without a doubt that it was show time again.

I was mad at first. How come Jake got to stay home, eating my hay, with a mare for company, when I had to get cleaned up, and made to perform tricks? It just didn't seem fair. So I ran from Daisy when she came out with my halter. I couldn't go far but I wanted her to know I was not happy. I ran, I kicked, and I screamed at her. Then I made a mistake: I turned around and saw the look of disappointment on Daisy's face. This show meant a lot to her. If she was willing to come out of retirement to show how much we had learned, I guess I could, too. I dropped my head and stopped running to let her walk up to me and catch me. I didn't even put up a fuss getting on the trailer this time. I had a job to do for Daisy.

*****

Our first class was Showmanship. I thought it was a bit silly, walking around leading Daisy, but it seemed important to her. Daisy cleaned up nicely too. If she weren't my human and I didn't know her smell above all others, I may not have recognized her. She sparkled from head to toe. From the waist down, she wore all black, to match my coat. From the waist up, she wore red, to match my saddle pad. We were a fine looking pair.

Before we went in, Wendy coached Daisy and me on our pattern. "Above all, look at the judge."

Got it. I can drill holes in him with my eyes.

"And don't forget to smile. Remember you're proud to be here."

Smile? How in the world do you expect me to smile? I'm a horse. We can't smile. Oh, you must mean Daisy. She does have a nice smile.

Lost in my thoughts, I didn't realize it was time to go in the arena until I felt Daisy tugging on my halter. We jogged down to where the judge was standing and Daisy froze. I could tell she was nervous.

Come on, Daisy. Snap out of it.

165

I tried to nudge her. She dodged my snout and turned to face the judge, smiling all the while. That was all she did. In her nervousness she had forgotten our pattern. It was up to me to save this class. I tried to make our turn, but with Daisy frozen to the spot, she didn't remember that's what we were supposed to do. So I backed up. That did the trick. Daisy remembered we were supposed to turn, and then the rest of our pattern went smoothly.

We lined up to watch the rest of the horses and their humans; their humans did better than mine. It was Daisy's first show, so I'm sure her nerves had something to do with it. I understand. I was nervous during my first show, too. It seemed like a lifetime ago.

When the horses were done, the voice in the sky started talking. I perked up when I heard Daisy's name, but the horse they announced was 'Cobby', so at first I figured there was another human called Daisy. Then the voice in the sky corrected the name, 'Kobi'.

Cobby? Really? At least they finally figured it out. Sheesh - Cobby.

Shaking my head in disbelief, I led Daisy out of the arena to get our ribbon.

Our next class was a trail class. I figured we would do pretty well since Daisy and I go trail riding all the time together. Boy, was I wrong! It was nothing like what we do in the woods. The gate was the most difficult thing to do. First of all, it wasn't a real gate. A real gate we could have handled, no problem. This one looked like a green snake draped across two posts. Daisy was to lift one end of the snake, hold on to it as we walked between the posts, and then place the snake back in its original spot. The only thing no one counted on was whether or not horses wanted the green snake coming over their heads. I guess other horses were okay with it; I was not. Anytime that snake would come close, I would throw myself in reverse, backing up until Daisy let go of it.

Daisy, what are you thinking? I don't want anything coming up over my head. I never would have survived in the wild if I did. Remember, I'm not your average horse, I'm a mustang! Come on, drop it, and let's move on to the rest of the course.

Daisy has a stubborn streak. As long as the judge would allow her to try it, she did. I could have just done the right thing, and let her hook the snake on the post, but then again I didn't want anyone thinking it would be alright to always bring something strange up and over my head. I had to make a stand, so after ten minutes of backing up, I convinced all humans present it was time to move on. We did the rest of the course perfectly, but Daisy was exhausted after that and we still had two more classes to go.

Next up was our pleasure class. Daisy had to show the world, or at least everyone at the show grounds, what a pleasure I was to ride. Now, that should have been easy. We've been working for years together, and I knew exactly what jog rhythm she likes the best: slow and easy. What we never saw coming were the other seven horses in this class. And at least five of them weren't what Wendy or Daisy would consider "green." Even though I gave it my best, we didn't place. The other horses and their humans were just a bit better than we were. It didn't seem fair. Those other horses seemed to have much more experience than we did. After that ride I was exhausted from showing off all day. I was ready to go home.

"Just one more class," Daisy said. "I need you to hold it together for one more class."

What Daisy didn't tell me is that we had to wait over an hour for it. That I couldn't do. I started getting antsy and dancing with impatience. Daisy wasn't paying attention. I wanted a break. I needed a break. I'm not proud of what I did next, but Daisy needed to understand that it was time to go home. I reared. Now it wasn't a full on, rest on my hocks, pawing at the sky with my front hooves, wild mustang kind of rear. It was more of a jump, only instead of all four hooves coming off of the ground, it was just the front two. It was more of a mini-rear, actually.

That got her attention, but not in the way I expected. I figured Daisy would understand it was time to go home, dismount, and lead me back to my stall. Wrong! Daisy figured I was bored and started spinning me in circles. That was almost the opposite of what I wanted to do. It got my attention, though, and I quit thinking about how miserable I was just waiting for our next class to start. Before I knew what was happening, we were lined up ready to go in the arena for our final class.

I was over being good. I was over letting Daisy just sit up there on my back, while I had to remember our patterns. So I pretended that I forgot everything. When I was to stop at a cone, I overstepped and then threw my head in the air when Daisy corrected me. When I was supposed to jog, I started a few steps after we were supposed to, and walked a few steps before I was asked to go back down to a walk. I was obnoxious and it worked. Afterwards, Daisy took me back to the barn, untacked me, and I walked right onto the trailer, ready to go home. Finally.

*****

I was never so glad to be heading home. It had been one of the longest, hottest, sweatiest days of my life. As soon as the trailer stopped outside of the gate, I recognized the tinkling sound of the chain being unlatched; I took in a deep breath. I was home.

I caught Jake's scent, his own combination of sweaty musk and the sickness in his hoof.

"Jake! Jake, I'm home!" I yelled from the trailer.

"Kobi? Is that you?" Jake rumbled. "I've missed you."

Even with that mare for company, Jake still missed me. What a great friend.

CHAPTER 13 — JAKE'S INCIDENT

Jake's mind started playing tricks on him. One night it was really bad. Daisy and Rex came out to put us up in our stalls for the night. Everything was normal. Bedtime went like it had every single night since we moved here. Daisy had given us our snack and was filling our water buckets, while Rex was tossing us enough hay to keep us content for a few hours.

"Should I put some powder on Jake's hoof?" Daisy asked.

"It can't hurt," Rex answered.

Daisy went into Jake's stall, like she had done hundreds of times before, and squatted down by his hooves to poof the powder on them like she had done hundreds of times before. All of a sudden, Jake was terrified. I could tell from the whites showing around his eyes that he didn't know where he was or that Daisy was still squatting almost underneath him, doctoring his hooves. All Jake knew at that moment in time was that something was under him, and he was spooked.

With my mouth full of hay, there was nothing I could do to stop Jake or warn Daisy. I just watched, helpless, as Jake acted as any horse would do with something unknown under their belly. He kicked at it.

In his panic, Jake wasn't able to aim his first kick correctly, which was a good thing for Daisy. Instead of his hoof connecting with the side of Daisy's head, he only knocked her with the top of his foot, knocking her off balance.

Rex heard the commotion and ran back into the barn. Cuzzin tried to get in the stall to protect Daisy, but Rex was there to pull him back from joining the melee. Unable to do anything to stop Jake from kicking again, or get Daisy out from under Jake's massive hooves, the three of us just watched as Daisy's self protective instincts kicked in.

Knocked off balance by the kick to her head, Daisy rolled over onto her hands and knees to scramble out from under the massive force of Jake's hooves. He managed to kick her one more time in her knee, spinning her onto her back. She immediately flipped back over and crawled backwards the rest of the way to safety, to the back of Jake's stall.

With Jake's immediate danger gone, and no more threat under his belly, Jake stopped kicking. I think he realized what had just happened. It wasn't something that was going to kill him or even hurt him. He had just attacked Daisy.

The far, darkened corner of Jake's stall was quiet. What had happened to Daisy?

"What's going on in there? Talk to me, Daisy."

Please start talking. Jake didn't mean to hurt you. Get up and be okay.

"I'm fine. Don't talk to me for a minute. I need to see what's hurt."

I'm sure Daisy was only quiet for a few seconds, but it seemed like an eternity until she spoke again.

"My knee hurts really bad, but I can move it, so it's probably not broken. My head hurts, too, but nowhere near as bad as my knee."

"Just stay down. I'll come and help you up."

"Give me a minute to catch my breath first."

Always thinking of Jake and me before thinking about herself, Daisy asked, "Can you finish powdering Jake's hoof first? Just let him know what you are doing before you get down there so he doesn't get scared again."

When Rex was finished powdering Jake's hoof, he went back in to the stall to help Daisy to her feet. "What happened?" She asked, when she was standing up again. "I heard you yell at Cuzzin. Did he come in here and scare Jake?"

"No, it was you. Jake got scared with you being under him, and started kicking."

Holding on to the walls of the stall, Daisy slowly made her way out of Jake's stall.

"I'll close up Jake's stall, if you'll finish giving Kobi his hay," Daisy offered.

She turned around, holding onto the wall for support. As she clipped the chain together, closing up Jake's stall, she started weaving on her feet.

Rex, get in here. Daisy's going down!

I watched her fall in slow motion. As she was slipping down, she slammed her head against the thick wooden post outside of Jake's stall. Somehow she managed to catch her arm around another board, slowing down her descent. Rex saw what was going on and rushed over to her. He managed to get behind her so she didn't fall all the way to the ground, and hurt herself even more. He gently helped her sit down on the ground.

"I'm fine."

"No, you're not. You just passed out."

"Seriously, my head's okay. My knee really hurts, though."

Rex lifted up Daisy's pants leg, exposing her bloody knee.

"That's why. Jake banged you up pretty bad. We need to get you in the house to clean up your knee, and look at your head. You may need to go to the hospital."

Catching the metallic scent of Daisy's blood, Jake started blowing. He hadn't said a word since the incident happened, but knowing Jake's abusive history, I'm sure he was afraid that harsh hands would be beating him next. He still hadn't learned Daisy and Rex would never lift a hand in anger towards us.

"Before I get up, go pet Jake. Let him know everything's alright."

Rex went over to Jake, talking gently to him and rubbing his head. "It's okay, big guy. Everything's fine."

That seemed to calm Jake. He stopped blowing, went back to his hay, and starting eating.

Turning back to Daisy, Rex said, "Let's get you inside and away from the mosquitoes."

After things had quieted down and Daisy was safely in the house, Jake finally spoke. "Kobi? Do you think she's going to be okay?"

"Daisy's tough. I'm sure she'll be fine. What happened though?"

"I don't know. I got confused. I didn't know where I was. I thought something was about to attack my belly, and I needed to protect myself. So I started kicking. I never would have done it if I would have known it was Daisy. Really! You've got to believe me, Kobi. I never would hurt her on purpose."

"I know that."

"Do you think they know that? Do Daisy and Rex know I wouldn't hurt them on purpose?"

"They know. Don't worry about it. Daisy will be fine."

Even as I said those words, I wasn't too sure. She had taken a bad beating under Jake's massive hooves.

Breakfast was late the next morning. The sun was already up with no sign of anyone up in the house. Usually I would be a little more patient, but after last night's incident, I was worried about Daisy. I saw a light come on in the bathroom.

"Daisy, is that you? Are you up? Are you okay?" I yelled.

Cuzzin started barking from inside the house. *Stupid dog.*

"Shh! I'll be out there in a minute." Daisy said.

I quieted down. I heard Daisy's voice. She was okay. Everything was going to be fine.

*****

It turned out everything wasn't fine. While Daisy was on the mend, Jake was getting worse. He couldn't come out of the back yard to graze anymore. His feet hurt worse than ever. The air surrounding him reeked of sickness. Jake spent much more time lying down. When he could stand up to graze, he would stretch his neck out as far as he could reach, nibbling grass, before moving his feet forward. I realized that soon Jake wouldn't be able to stand up anymore. It made me sad.

I wasn't the only one. Rex and Daisy were worried about Jake, too.

At bedtime, I would come trotting up. I loved going into my stall at night. There was nothing to worry about. Predators couldn't come in and Daisy always made sure we had a snack and enough hay to last almost until morning. It was the perfect way to end every day grazing in the sunshine.

Poor Jake, though. At bedtime, he would start coming in: leaning back on his haunches, then throwing himself forward - projecting his front feet forward. It was a painful and time consuming process for everyone, horse and human alike. Rex and Daisy never gave up on Jake, though. While Rex was in charge of making sure Jake and I had enough hay, Daisy would be out with Jake, encouraging him to move forward with his favorite treat, Cheerios. She'd give him a handful of it and then walk backwards a few steps to persuade Jake to follow her for another mouthful. It took some time to get him in, but it was effective.

"Kobi," Jake said one night, after an especially long, hot day. "I'm tired."

"I know," I said, chewing on my hay. "You laid down a lot today."

"My feet hurt all the time now. Not even the medicine Daisy puts in my food helps anymore. I'd lie down all the time if I didn't get so hungry. I don't know what to do."

"I don't either. I bet Daisy and Rex aren't out of ideas yet. Let's see what they have for you tomorrow."

I'm not sure when Daisy started understanding what Jake and I were saying to each other, but the next day the vet came out to see Jake.

I'm always protective of Jake when the vet comes out. I don't like to see my large friend in pain. Daisy put me in my stall so I couldn't interfere. Jake was already standing next to my stall wall, so I was still able to see and hear everything that was happening.

"We can't do anything more for him," the vet said.

What? Why not? There's got to be something you haven't tried yet.

"You guys have done a great job with him. You've done all that you could. Jake just has too many things going against him now, between the canker in his left foot, the founder in his right, not to mention the possibility of Cushing's disease. You've kept him around six months longer that I believed possible. You gave him your best and he's had a great run. Since the pain meds aren't keeping him comfortable anymore, I recommend you put him down."

Daisy sobbed and nodded. Hearing her heart break almost broke mine. She put her arms around Jake's neck and cried. Since she was whispering into Jake's thick mane, I couldn't hear everything she told him, but I caught the end.

"I'm so sorry, Jake. I did everything I could. Now you won't hurt anymore."

As Daisy moved away, Jake moved his nose over to touch mine.

"Jake, you're going to be okay. Daisy will think of something."

"Not this time. I don't want Daisy to try anything else. I'm tired. My feet hurt. I can barely walk anymore. It's time, my friend. Take care of Daisy and Rex for me. They are good humans."

I couldn't stand to hear Jake talk like that…like he was giving up. So I did the only thing I knew to do, I nipped at his mouth; to get him quiet, and to let him know I cared for him.

Daisy grabbed the bright yellow box of treats that Jake loves so much, and with the group of humans following, led Jake to the front pasture. As he limped away, I knew I was seeing Jake's massive hindquarters move away from me for the last time.

"Jake!"

He didn't answer me.

I saw the horse trailer pull through the front gate and knew it was coming for me. I heard Wendy telling Daisy she felt it would be best if I went to her place for a bit. I didn't want to go, but knew I didn't have a choice in the matter either.

One of the girls from Wendy's barn hopped out of the truck and headed straight to my stall. Everyone else was still surrounding Jake. She grabbed my halter from the hook next to my stall, haltered me up, and led me to the waiting trailer. She took me the long way, all the way around the house, far from where Jake and the others were standing. I took one last look before I walked onto the trailer. I saw Rex with his arm around

Daisy, her shoulders shaking from sobbing, and Jake looking up as he finished the last bite of his favorite treat.

I turned back and walked onto the trailer.

Goodbye, Jake. You were the best friend and brother a horse could ever ask for.

CHAPTER 14: NEW BEGINNINGS

When I backed out of the trailer, I found myself back at Wendy's barn. The short trip gave me time to work myself up into a snit. I was mad. I know Daisy wanted me at Wendy's so I could be with other horses, but I didn't want to be here. I wanted to be back at home. With Jake. With Daisy. With Rex. They are my family, the ones who needed me now, not Wendy.

I was put in a stall and left alone. I paced and wondered what was going to happen next. Before it was dinner time, Daisy came to see me. I knew she was upset and had been crying, her eyes were blood red and so puffy I don't know how she could see out of them. I walked up and nuzzled her. I wanted her to know I was still here. I still loved her.

She scratched my ears. "Oh, Kobi," she cried, "What in the world are we going to do now?"

I didn't have any idea what she was talking about. I knew Jake was not going to be home when I got there, and I would never see my brother again, so that was probably what Daisy meant. What I didn't understand was why this was different than any other time we spent together? Daisy and I always did what came naturally to us and enjoyed ourselves.

Why should now be any different?

I found out soon enough Daisy wasn't there to take me back home. She came to see me several times a day, though. She fed me breakfast, came later to ride, then again to feed me dinner, and sometimes even came once it was dark just to scratch my ears and talk to me. It reminded me of those times in prison with Wade when he scratched my ears and just talked to me.

I'll admit this now, but when I was spending time at Wendy's barn, I was not a nice horse. Oh, I still behaved great for Daisy and loved her every time she came out. I was even half-way decent for Wendy. When it came to other horses, though, let's just say I was a complete jerk. I didn't want to be there. I didn't want to spend time with any other horse but Jake. They just didn't get it. Each time Wendy would put a different horse out to pasture with me, I would see just how long it would take until Wendy took them away. Usually it was just a few minutes until I had either kicked or bit the other horse bloody and into submission. Then Wendy would come running, yell at me, and remove the other horse. If I couldn't be with Jake, I wanted to be alone.

Unfortunately for me, Daisy didn't want me to be alone. One evening when Wendy was walking past my stall, I heard her tell Daisy, "I don't know what to do. He attacks every horse we put with him. I don't know what other horse to try with him."

"Oh, Kobi," Daisy sighed. "You have to give someone a chance. It's not good for you to be alone. It's not good for me if you are alone either; I'd worry about you all the time. Please, give one of these horses a chance. I know they will never take Jake's place. They never can. But for me, please, let one come home with us."

I didn't want to. But because Daisy cried every time she came to see me, I tried. They decided a mare might be the best match for me during this rough time. So as I loaded back up on the trailer to go home, I looked over and saw that a small, dappled brown Morgan mare called Kya was loaded on beside me.

Oh, great, a mare. The things I put up with for Daisy.

It was strange pulling up the driveway and not hearing Jake's rumble to welcome me home. I knew why he wasn't there and was trying my best to accept it, but it was tough. I was glad to see Rex come out to greet us. It was nice to know some things were still the same.

I was also happy when I saw Daisy was keeping Kya in a different pasture. She didn't seem too bad, but after the crazy experiences I've had with mares, like Loco and Malevolent, and after just losing my best friend, I wasn't in the mood to deal with another mare. Besides, she was a talker. I never got a moment of quiet to be with my own thoughts.

"Kobi? Where are you?" Kya hollered.

"I'm up front."

A few minutes later, I'd hear the same question.

"Kobi? Where are you?"

"Over here."

This went on every few minutes, for hours. I was trying to be nice. I had promised Daisy I would give another horse a chance, but after a while I couldn't take it anymore.

"Oh, Kobi,"

"Leave me alone!" I yelled back.

I guess I was a little loud, because Daisy took my scream to mean I was lonely. She actually put Kya in my pasture with me. If I only would have kept my mouth shut and ignored that silly mare. If I only I hadn't yelled. I would have had some peace and quiet. As soon as that mare joined me, any hope I had of spending time alone that night was gone.

I made the best of an imperfect situation. Whenever Kya was close by, I would start grooming her neck and withers, so that she'd also scratch all my itchy spots. It worked great for a few days, and while I would never admit it, I was beginning to think Wendy had made a good choice sending Kya home with me. She was turning into a comforting companion after all.

As soon as that thought left my head, Kya turned and looked at me. "I don't like Daisy," she said out of the blue.

What? How could anyone not like Daisy? What was she going to say next, the grass is too green?

I stopped chewing the mouthful of hay in my mouth, turned to face her, and pinned my ears. "Why not?"

"Oh, I don't know," Kya said, starting to change her mind now that I confronted her. "She's not around all the time, and when she is, I don't think she's all that nice." Kya's argument was starting to build up speed. "She yells at me a lot too."

"The only reason Daisy yells at you is because you don't listen to her. She's trying to teach you how things are done at our barn."

"Well, I don't like it here. I think you'd be happier back at my old barn, with me."

"Without Daisy?" I asked.

"Definitely without Daisy."

That was all the silly mare needed to say. I couldn't imagine life without Daisy, and hope I never needed to. Daisy was *my* human. If Kya couldn't understand that, our friendship was over. I stretched my neck out, bared my teeth, and bit her.

Kya squealed. "Stop it! You're mad because you know I'm right." Kya started to move away from me, "Daisy isn't that great. I think she likes that dog better than you, too."

I'd had enough of that mare and her mouth. I ran her down. She tried to run away. Anytime I would get within biting distance, I would snap my jaws. Sometime they would click and come up with nothing, other times I would get a piece of her ribs or hindquarters and really nip her.

Daisy came running out of the house. "Kobi! Stop!" She jumped over the fence, into the pasture and tried to separate us. Kya almost ran Daisy over – twice! Each time Kya got too close to Daisy, I would step up my attack, screaming, "Leave Daisy alone!"

I finally got Kya to run into a tight corner, where she couldn't run from me anymore. I knew Daisy would come soon to separate us, so I took full advantage of the time I had and stayed behind Kya, pushing her deeper in the corner, biting her in the hindquarters. "Don't ever talk about Daisy again!"

"Kobi, what's gotten in to you?" Daisy snatched me by my fly mask and led me back to the barn and into time-out. "You can't behave this way."

As soon as I was out of the corner, Kya came out and ran past us gloating with her tail held high. "She's such a weak human."

I twisted my head, breaking out of Daisy's grasp, and pursued Kya again. It didn't last too long this time. Daisy grabbed my fly mask as I sailed past her and spun me back to her.

"Kobi, you're being bad. You don't behave this way. What's wrong with you?"

You don't understand. She was saying hateful things about you.

"Come on. You have to go to your stall and calm down." She led me into the barn. I knew she didn't understand what was going on. I did my time out without a fuss, knowing I had done what I needed to do in order to defend my Daisy.

My relationship with Kya deteriorated after that. Anytime she would see me in the pasture, she would walk up and say something nasty under her breath. If I didn't see Daisy and Rex around, I would bite her. Sometimes I would get caught and either get yelled at or put in my stall for awhile. The punishment was worth it.

Daisy was concerned for Kya's safety around me. She asked Wendy to come and take Kya back home with her.

Good! Finally, some peace and quiet around here.

When I saw the horse trailer with Kya's dappled rump in it pull away from the property, I ran victory laps around the pasture.

"It's okay. We'll find you a good pasture mate, one that you actually like this time." Daisy said as she put her arms around my neck after I had run myself into a good lather. "It might just take us some time."

Take all the time you need. I have you and I have Rex. Another horse is just a bonus.

*****

We got into a different routine. It wasn't the same without Jake, and we were struggling to find a new normal for our lives. The only one who seemed unaffected by the loss of Big Jake was the world's dumbest dog, Cuzzin. But even he and I came to a truce.

One sunny afternoon, Daisy was being especially playful. She had let Cuzzin out and he was sniffing around the back pasture. I came up to the fence to nuzzle her.

"Go get Cuzzin," Daisy whispered, with a twinkle in her eye.

What? You always yell at me when I chase him.

"Go get Cuzzin," she whispered again, a smile tugged at the corners of her mouth.

I turned to see where the offending dog was. "Go get him."

I spun around, zeroed in on the dog, and took off after him.

Cuzzin always loves this game. I'd chase him, running and spinning back on my hindquarters, and then he pretends to chase me. Whenever he gets too close, I kick up my heels, always making sure not to hit the goofy dog. When the game goes on too long, I chase him to a fence and he always ducks under, leaving the pasture and the game behind.

We played the game like we always do. Everyone seemed to be enjoying the chase, when out of nowhere, Cuzzin decided the game was over and ran toward the fence. Except he didn't duck to slip under the board, like he usually does. Instead, he ran, full speed, head on, into the fence board. The game ended with a loud *thud*. Cuzzin whined for a second, got up, shook his head, and walked away.

Oh, I hope I don't get blamed for that. I wasn't even chasing him when he did that.

Daisy started laughing, a sound I hadn't heard much since we lost Jake.

"Did Kobi finally get Cuzzin?" Rex asked from inside the garage.

"No," Daisy laughed. "You know how Cuzzin ducks under the fence when he feels Kobi is about to catch him? Well, this time he didn't duck." Daisy was laughing so hard she couldn't finish the story.

Rex came around the corner, "We always knew he was the world's dumbest dog."

"And he was being chased by the world's smartest horse. He didn't stand a chance," Daisy said, as she walked away, still laughing.

It was really funny. I stayed in a good mood the rest of that day, until I saw another horse trailer pull into the yard and stop. I could smell another mare.

Another mare? Seriously? Daisy, didn't you learn anything from the last one?

But when the new mare backed off the trailer and turned to look at me, I was speechless. She was the prettiest mare I had seen since leaving Nevada.

CHAPTER 15 — SUGAR

Daisy led this new horse, this beautiful new paint mare, up to our barn. Daisy had left me in my stall after dinner, and now I knew it was to make introductions easier.

"Kobi, this is Sugar. She's your new pasture mate, so be nice and mind your manners."

"Hello, Sugar." I nickered, "Glad to have you here."

Sugar ignored me. She was much more interested in the new sights, sounds, and the grass her new home held for her, than talking to me.

That's okay. She'll come around. I'm the only other horse she can talk to.

It didn't take Sugar long before her brown and white nose peeked over my stall wall.

"Is it just the two of us?" She was soft-spoken; her voice was calm and quiet.

"Horses? Yeah, we're the only two out here." I moved my nose over to touch hers, "I'm Kobi."

"Nice to meet you, Kobi," We sniffed each other over the stall wall. "As you've heard already, I'm Sugar."

Ahhh, Sugar. I hope you're as sweet as your name.

*****

Over the next few days, Sugar and I got to know each other. I was pleased to see she wasn't as needy as Kya. I was able to go to a different part of the pasture without her screaming in panic. The only time I ever saw Sugar panic was when Daisy took me away to work me in the front field. But after the second or third time, Sugar knew I would be coming back to her, so she quieted down.

Since she wasn't much of a talker, it took some prompting to get her story out of her. One afternoon Sugar and I were in our stalls while an afternoon storm raged above us. Since sharing stories over hay worked to get Jake's story out, I tried it with Sugar.

"So, Sugar, where are you from?"

"Originally, or just my last home?"

"How many homes have you had?"

"I've lost track. I've lived with some humans more than once, some humans for a very long time, and some for only a few weeks. I try not to get too attached to anyone anymore. They don't stick around long."

"Why not? What happens to make you move?" Did she do anything to her humans to make them get rid of her, or did she just have bad luck with them? Were Daisy and Rex in danger with this gorgeous creature?

"I'm not sure. It's not like I'm mean or anything. I've never hurt my human or left them behind. After a while they just start to ignore me and then I'm out of a home again. I overheard the last humans I lived with saying that I was too big. You believe that? Too big to ride." She dropped her nose to her hay, taking another bite, trying to end the discussion.

"You don't have to worry about that here. Once Daisy and Rex choose you as their horse, they keep you forever. There's nothing they won't do for you."

Sugar didn't say another word, so I told her all about Jake and his issues, as well as my history with Daisy and Rex. By the time I was finished, the sun was beginning to set, but the storm was still raging above us. Daisy had already come to feed us dinner and toss us our after dinner hay. We were in for a long night, so I tried to get Sugar talking again.

"Since you've had so many humans, I bet you've seen and learned a lot of different things."

"Hmph! You're right, I have. I haven't seen anything as bad as your friend Jake, though. The humans I've had mostly leave me be, except for an occasional trail ride, and then for whatever reason, move me out again. I don't think I'm a bad horse. I just don't understand why I can't keep a human."

Now that Sugar started talking again, she seemed to need to get her story out. Almost to reassure herself, and convince me, that she wasn't a bad horse. She was just a victim of uncaring humans.

She was born in a small town in a place called "Georgia." Her mother and father were both Paints, even though she never actually met her father. She was born at a breeding barn, so she was able to grow and frolic with many colts and fillies her own age. As soon as she was old enough to be weaned, she and all the other foals were sold and sent off to their first homes, to make room for the next batch of foals that were soon to be born.

She was sold, with a couple of her friends, to a trainer. There she learned her ground manners. The trainer started by teaching her to let humans groom every inch of her, including her belly and her legs, and to wear a halter without complaining. From there her education went to learning riding commands, through my least favorite activity in the world – lunging. Sugar didn't mind any of it, though. She wanted to make her humans happy. Even when it was time to saddle, bridle, and ride her, Sugar didn't mind. In fact, she enjoyed spending time in the woods so much that she looked forward to each ride. When her training was almost complete, she was sold again.

She went through a series of owners. Most of them were kind to her, and rode her a lot in the beginning, but after awhile each owner's enthusiasm for her shrank and she was ignored. The reasons for her being sold were as numerous as her owners: humans going back to school, growing apart through divorce, having a baby and preferring the baby's attention over horses, humans losing their jobs and not having the money to feed her, or getting new jobs and not having the time to spend with her. It didn't seem to matter the reason, the end result was always the same: Sugar was sold again.

Before coming to Daisy's, her last home was her favorite. She'd been rescued from a family who had recently broken up and divorced. Somehow, someway, Sugar was forgotten about again. While not being physically abused, like Jake had been, she was a victim just the same. She was given hay once or twice a day and then left to her own devices. Her hooves were ignored, she wasn't groomed, she wasn't loved.

One of her former trainers found her. She remembered what a good and quiet horse Sugar has always been and rescued her from her loneliness and neglect. Sugar was excited to have a job again. Her new home was a place where humans in need could come and find comfort in horses. Some of the humans had physical problems, some had emotional problems. They would come out, groom the horses, and talk to them. It gave everyone, horses and humans alike, a purpose. It was eerily similar to Wade and me.

While Sugar's calm and easy going, she is a tall animal. Her size alone scared some of the people seeking comfort, and it wasn't too long before Sugar was left in her stall while all of the other horses went to work. She was beginning to see the cycle repeat itself yet again.

I told her that her constant traveling was over as of the day she backed out of the trailer and found her new home here. While Sugar will never replace Jake, she seemed to be a good friend. She actually has a lot of Jake's mannerisms which helped keep his memory alive. She rumbles in the morning for her breakfast, she always turns and waits for cookies after being turned out, and is the most food motivated animal I've ever seen, after Jake himself, of course.

It's different. It's not better and it's certainly not worse – and life has to, and must, go on. We've eased into a new sense of normal now. Daisy and Rex spend more time with us, riding the trails and back woods of Florida. Each day their sadness is lifted

a little bit more. I've finally stopped looking for my big, bay Percheron friend across the breezeway, and now find comfort in Sugar's painted body.

Life has become calm and quiet again, but I know it won't last too long. Daisy becomes bored and restless with too much routine. It won't be long before I see Wendy pull up again, and know that another show is right around the corner. For now, I'm going to spend my days grazing with Sugar, chasing Cuzzin, and enjoying trail rides with Daisy on my back and Rex riding Sugar beside me.

And that's my story.

Epilogue

Kobi's story is based on his real-life events. Every person and every animal's name has been changed except for the big stars: Kobi, Big Jake, and Sugar.

Researching Kobi's past has proved to be an interesting journey for both of us. Thanks to the phenomenal record-keeping, his freeze brand, and their willingness to share their information with me, the United States Bureau of Land Management (BLM) pieced together all of Kobi's past, from his actual round-up and capture in the plains of Nevada until his adoption in Jacksonville, Florida.

The BLM stepped in on the horses' behalf in 1971. That was when Congress established the Wild-Free Roaming Horse and Burro Act which declared that "...wild free-roaming horses and burros are living symbols of the historic and pioneer spirit of the West...." The Act gives the BLM the authority to manage, protect and control any wild horse or burro that is unbranded, unclaimed, and free-roaming found on public lands.

When the Act was first established, there were over 25,000 wild horses and burros on the western plains. Now there are over 38,000. The BLM controls the population through fertility control, and has given the vaccine to nearly 3,000 mares, with no significant change in herd sizes. Herds double their population every four years, so there are annual round-ups, with the same herd being rounded up every three to five years. The land that the horses roam can sustain about 27,000 horses and burros. Since there are over 38,000 horses and burros roaming there now, there is risk of overgrazing, leading to animal starvation. Thus the need for round-ups and adoptions. Since the program was established, the BLM has placed over 217,000 horses and burros in private homes. Like mine.

All of the mustangs captured by the BLM are freeze-branded with a unique code. As the name suggests, freeze-branding does not use the traditional and painful methods of hot branding, but instead uses liquid nitrogen to freeze the skin a few seconds, branding the horse with little pain. Each freeze-brand starts with the characters US, which is unique to the Bureau's mustangs. Following the 'US' is a pattern of symbols, which indicate the horse's year of birth, and a unique six-digit serial number.

Based on Kobi's freeze brand and serial number, 02585761, the BLM was able to tell me he was born on the Nevada plains during 2002. He was captured in December 2003. In January 2004, he was sent to Palomino Valley Preparatory in Nevada. Palomino Valley is a 160-acre holding pen to separate the mustangs as well as to give them their freeze-brand, vaccines, de-worming, and hoof trimming. From June until September he did time in the Hutchinson Correctional Facility in Kansas. After his release, he was sent to Pauls Valley, Oklahoma to a 400-acre holding pen where he stayed until he was sent to the Jackson, Mississippi Field Office for adoption placement in February 2005. The Jackson Field Office sent Kobi to Jacksonville, Florida, where he was adopted in a matter of days.

Ever since he "became" Kobi, as described in Chapter 6, I have had the honor of being his human. This book tells the story of our journey together, and most of the ups and downs that we went through. While I don't think I would want to make the journey all over again (especially the falls and the bruised ribs), I wouldn't change a thing! It has been an exciting and rewarding ride together. Kobi is a remarkable horse.

Kobi's story is mostly true but Jake's story, on the other hand, is mostly fiction. It is a fact, however, that Jake was a rescue who had seen a good deal of abuse. The notch in his neck was real, as were the scars that were scattered along most of his body. He did originate out of Kentucky in a region known for using draft horses for logging purposes. Aside from all that, Jake's real story was known only to him. Like Kobi, Jake found his forever home with me. Also true was our painful battle with canker and founder that we lost in April 2011. Jake was an amazing horse. He had many friends who supported us both physically and emotionally during that six-month ordeal. I like to think that he is frolicking up in horse heaven right now, away from the Florida heat, bugs, and most of all, his bad hooves. I love you, Jake.

Sugar entered our lives a few weeks after Jake left. She is as sweet as her name implies but doesn't take any of Kobi's temper tantrums. She puts him back in his place pretty quick. Her story is also mostly fiction. It surprised me how much easier it was to track a wild horse's history than one who has been owned privately. Based on her papers, she has gone through several homes in her eleven-year life, and was briefly used for equine therapy before finding her forever home with us.

My Kobi. He truly is as amazing in real life as he is in the book, and only another "horse person" or maybe only another "mustang person" can appreciate most of his unusual and endearing personality. At 14.2 hands high, he is a small horse (even though he doesn't think so)!

His love for humans has always amazed me and has led me to believe that all of his contact with us humans has been positive.

The first time I met him, he won my heart by sucking on my fingers. I am fortunate enough to be greeted by his whinnies every time he sees me. Not too many other horses will do those things, only the special ones!

Not to say Kobi can't be exasperating at times. It is difficult to stay warm around him in winter. If he sees anyone wearing clothing with a zipper, he feels it's his job to unzip it for you. He unties shoelaces, too. And when it rains, I can't seem to get him off of the front porch, simply because he still can't stand getting wet. It's amazing the amount of stuff he's broken on the porch with his hind end!

This is Kobi's story, as told by him.

For more information about the Bureau of Land Management or the Wild Horse and Burro Adoption Program, visit their website at: wildhorseandburro.blm.gov.

About the author:

Heather Hamel is an author, horse trainer, and teacher. While working her way through college to become a teacher, she discovered a passion for storytelling, while working as a ghost tour guide in the historic and haunted town of St. Augustine, Florida.

After teaching for a few years, Heather could not shake storytelling. Today, she teaches and tutors students with dyslexia, as well as finds time to write at 5:00 am. She has written on-line horse articles, two middle grade novels, and is currently working on a four book crypto-zoological series for her middle grade readers.

Website: http://HeatherHamel.com

About the artist:

Jean Drayovitch is a native Floridian who grew up among orange blossoms and shell paved roads, Jean developed a love for Florida's natural beauty at an early age. As a girl scout attending horse camp, Jean garnered attention when she drew a perfect anatomical horse diagram complete with grooming supplies. Horses would remain a key subject in Jean's artwork for years.

Currently Jean resides in downtown St. Augustine. With murals and paintings regularly on display in local establishments, Jean continues to make her mark on the Old City. In 2011, she and another artist founded the Anonymous Society of Artists to network with other local artists. This group meets weekly to draw and paint together and encourage its participants to reach their full potential as artists.

Website: http://www.jeandrayovitch.com/

Acknowledgements:

This book is a culmination of many things: blood, sweat, tears, and support! So many people helped along the way, so here it goes in no particular order, except in my scattered mind:

Les Clements, my love (after the horses). Thank you for supporting all of my crazy, half-thought out plans, starting with: "I think I want to get back into horses," to "I think I want to write a book," and every stage in between. You have encouraged me when I sat there crying, both while training Kobi and writing about those training experiences. You listened to my excited ramblings after talking to the BLM, and just smiled and nodded. Without you, this book never would have happened, and without you, Kobi may never have happened!

A very special thanks also goes to Lynda Mangalls, for giving us the lead on a black horse who was for sale.

Roy Gulick. What can I say? Without your help and guidance though the grammatical world that I found myself floundering in, all would have been lost!

Toni Oliva. Another person who without your help and unending support I never would have finished. You've read every change and version and supported me (and Kobi) throughout most of his story. Thank you, thank you, thank you!

Jean Drayovitch. The cover art is perfect. How you captured Kobi's essence from his soulful eyes to his playful lip I'll never know – you are amazing!

Mom and dad, without you passing on the love of reading and love of horses – this dream never would have happened in the first place.

And finally a heart-felt thank you to everyone who read through Kobi's stories, reminding me of things I had forgotten and helping with corrections even after the 200th read-through: Emily, Sandra, Melissa, Susie, Jodi, Cheri, Lila. It takes a village.

Finally, a huge thank you to the Bureau of Land Management. If it were not for your Wild Horse Adoption Program, there would not be a story! While researching Kobi's past, every person that I spoke with, in every department that I called, was eager and willing to help me with my project. I remember laughing along with your personnel the day I found out that Kobi spent three months in a penitentiary. Not to mention when I found out that the competitive bidding wasn't all that exciting: the bidding started at $125 and he sold for $135! Thank you for being on this journey with us. Special thanks for the BLM go out to: Debbie C. in National Marketing, Timothy G. at the Palomino Valley, Lauren with the Jackson Field Office, and Jackie with the Department of Corrections at the Hutchinson Correctional Facility. Your information was invaluable!

Other books by Heather Hamel:

Horse Books:

Kobi: Memoirs of a Mustang

Sugar: My Journey Home

Ghostly Mysteries:

Murder of Crows

Destruction of Wild Cat (Halloween 2016 release)

Cryptozoology Series

Within Emerald Forests (Book 1)

Under Sapphire Skies (Book 2)

Beneath Diamond Waters (Book 3)

Across Ruby Fields (Book 4)

Thank you so much for reading Kobi's story, I hope you

enjoyed it. Please let me know what you thought!

-Heather Hamel

Contact me at: heather.hamel@hotmail.com or through her website, www.HeatherHamel.com and don't forget to leave a review on Amazon and Good Reads!

www.ingramcontent.com/pod-product-compliance
Lightning Source LLC
Chambersburg PA
CBHW031545040426
42452CB00006B/199